DESIGN AS SCHOLARSHIP

For researchers in the learning sciences community, there is a lack of literature on current design practice and its many obstacles. *Design as Scholarship: Case Studies from the Learning Sciences* is an informative resource that addresses this need by providing instructive reference points and guidelines for successful projects. Drawing from the reflections of diverse practitioners and thorough case studies, this text guides readers in understanding the research in the context of their own work. It touches upon educational technologies, community co-design, and more, and is grounded in the critical analysis of experts seeking to grow the community.

Vanessa Svihla is an Assistant Professor in Organization, Information and Learning Sciences (OI&LS) at the University of New Mexico.

Richard Reeve is an Assistant Professor in Information and Communication Technology in Teaching and Learning in the Faculty of Education at Queen's University, Canada.

DESIGN AS ...

DESIGN AS SCHOLARSHIP

Case Studies from the Learning Sciences

*Edited by Vanessa Svihla
and Richard Reeve*

NEW YORK AND LONDON

First published 2016
by Routledge
711 Third Avenue, New York, NY 10017

and by Routledge
2 Park Square, Milton Park, Abingdon, Oxon, OX14 4RN

Routledge is an imprint of the Taylor & Francis Group, an informa business

Library of Congress Cataloging-in-Publication Data
Names: Svihla, Vanessa, editor.
Title: Design as scholarship : case studies from the learning sciences / edited by Vanessa Svihla and Richard Reeve.
Description: New York, NY : Routledge, 2016.
Identifiers: LCCN 2015034988 | ISBN 9781138891654 (hardback) | ISBN 9781138891661 (pbk.) | ISBN 9781315709550 (e-book)
Subjects: LCSH: Learning, Psychology of—Research—Case studies.
Classification: LCC LB1060 .D39 2016 | DDC 370.15/23—dc23
LC record available at http://lccn.loc.gov/2015034988

ISBN: 978-1-138-89165-4 (hbk)
ISBN: 978-1-138-89166-1 (pbk)
ISBN: 978-1-315-70955-0 (ebk)

Typeset in Bembo
by Apex CoVantage, LLC

CONTENTS

the local project. In the trial-and-error process that comprises DBR, some things are going to be productive and others are not. The failures, one might hope, might tell us something about how learning works. As Cobb, Confrey, diSessa, Lehrer, and Schauble (2003) elaborated, DBR involves

> both "engineering" particular forms of learning and systematically study-
> ing those forms of learning within the context defined by the means of
> supporting them. This designed context is subject to test and revision, and
> the successive iterations that result play a role similar to that of systematic
> variation in experiment.
>
> *(p. 9)*

This is the sense in which these iterations are referred to as design *experiments*. And, as with any experiment, we need to have a clear idea of how the experiment was conducted or, said in another way, we need to find a way to *document* the exploratory process underlying DBR.

The challenge in doing this kind of documentation work brings to mind what Harold Garfinkel, the American sociologist, described as the "Shop Floor Problem" (Garfinkel, 2002; Garfinkel & Liberman, 2007). Garfinkel first encountered the Shop Floor Problem in lengthy discussions with a group of industrial engineering consultants at McDonnell Douglas. McDonnell Douglas was and remains a major player in the aeronautics industry, one that has had, from time to time, to lay off workers when business was slow. The resulting fluctuations in staff were a source of trouble for a business that must meet very strict production standards. Thus, the consultants were brought in to document each of the jobs performed in the plant. What they discovered, however, was that, despite their best efforts, there was always a gap between what could be represented in the formal job descriptions and what the workers actually did.

Garfinkel recognized immediately that the problem was not unique to McDonnell Douglas, but was instead an instance of a much broader problem, one with profound implications for the social sciences. At its heart, the Shop Floor Problem is a problem of documentation. It turns on the question of what is to count as adequate description, whether in a manufacturer's standard operating procedure (SOP) or in a scientific report. With respect to doing ethnographic work at the worksite, it is the problem of specifying, from a worker's perspective, the nature of the work being performed. It requires determining for any particular job what makes it *that* job and no other. In the school of sociology he established, Garfinkel's Shop Floor Problem inspired several well-known investigations, including studies into what it is that makes the work of mathematicians mathematics (Livingston, 1986), what makes what a bench scientist does science (Lynch, 1985), and what makes playing on the piano jazz improvisation (Sudnow, 2001). These are challenging questions.

PREFACE

Timothy Koschmann

Through this book the authors and editors seek to engage a large and difficult question: What is the work of design and what is the nature of its scholarship? The designing in this case involves designing instructional artifacts and activities. There has been a long and well-established tradition within the learning sciences of employing iterative design-based methods. But although we seem to be growing more and more reliant on our work on such methods, we remain systematically inarticulate about the work of designing itself. As Vanessa Svihla and Richard Reeve report in the introductory chapter, what gets presented when learning scientists gather professionally are descriptions of design *products*, not descriptions of the aspirations, day-to-day challenges, and workaday experiences of the designers. The goal of this volume is to remedy that.

Why is it so important that we understand the work of designing instructional materials within design-based research (DBR)? It is because the design/test/re-design cycles of DBR are not only meant to lead to the production of a designed product, but are also intended to give us insight into learning itself. Consider the criteria for DBR work: the design of the theory of learning and the learning environment "are intertwined" (Design-Based Research Collective, 2003, p. 5); the process for doing such work occurs "through continuous cycles of design, enactment, analysis, and redesign"; this process leads to "sharable theories that help communicate relevant implications to practitioners and other educational designers"; these theories include a focus on "how designs function in authentic settings"; and the methods used to conduct this work "document and connect processes of enactment to outcomes of interest."

Drawing attention to the third item, we see that the design process is intended to yield not only product designs, but also "developing" theories pertaining to the nature of learning, theories that, presumably, have bearing that goes beyond

To enable us to learn something about learning from DBR, we need to find a way into the heads of the designers as they do their practical, everyday work of designing. We need to develop an intrinsic sense of the work being performed and, in so doing, come to better understand what makes tinkering with curricular materials designing. The studies that comprise this volume are offered as "worked examples," that is, problems in design worked to some state of completion. Though they are not necessarily written as "hybrid studies of work" (Garfinkel, 2002, pp. 100–103), all the chapters in this volume share with the studies mentioned earlier a common orientation to capturing the logic of the work at hand.

The emergence of a research literature that focuses on the nature of design in DBR is long overdue. If the DBR methodology is to flourish, we need to find a way to become more articulate about just what that methodology entails. The volume's title argues that design is not just a means to some more scholarly goal—for example, instructional innovation, perhaps, or educational reform—but is instead a legitimate form of scholarship in its own right. But *Design as Scholarship* also heralds a new form of scholarship, one that takes up the vernacular work practices of designers as its rightful object of study. This represents an important shift from the simple study of what works in the classroom to the study of what designers do when they are designing. By carefully studying such matters, we may eventually come to be more articulate about what learning's work itself entails.

Welcome to the shop floor!

References

Cobb, P., Confrey, J., diSessa, A., Lehrer, R., & Schauble, L. (2003). Design experiments in educational research. *Educational Researcher, 32*(1), 9–13.

Design-Based Research Collective. (2003). Design-based research: An emerging paradigm for educational inquiry. *Educational Researcher, 32*(1), 5–8.

Garfinkel, H. (2002). *Ethnomethodology's program: Working out Durkheim's aphorism.* Lanham, MD: Rowman & Littlefield.

Garfinkel, H., & Liberman, K. (2007). Introduction: The Lebenswelt origins of the sciences. *Human Studies, 30*, 3–7.

Livingston, E. (1986). *The ethnomethodological foundations of mathematics.* London: Routledge & Kegan Paul.

Lynch, M. (1985). *Art and artifact in laboratory science: A study of shop work and shop talk in a research laboratory.* London: Routledge & Kegan Paul.

Sudnow, D. (2001). *Ways of the hand: A rewritten account.* Cambridge, MA: MIT Press.

ACKNOWLEDGMENTS

The editors would like to acknowledge feedback on the idea for this book that came from attending and presenting at International Society of the Learning Sciences conferences. Part of the impetus for this book likewise came from having similar work rejected from such conferences.

1

UNTOLD STORIES

Vanessa Svihla and Richard Reeve

Overview

Learning scientists commonly report the design *of* an activity, object, or environment intended to produce some sort of learning or experience. The venues in which we publish typically do not encourage us to detail our designing as it occurred; this situation results in *final form* presentation of our work, which in turn leads to a picture of designing as deceptively straightforward. Worse, we argue, it provides little guidance about the reality of how researchers go about designing for learning. Those in the field are left to imagine how the process might have occurred and in turn are led to believe designing is simplistically phasic and linear. In addition, the siren call for the production and use of *design principles* in our work is symptomatic of the felt-need for more certainty in and about our designing. Even in our tradition of conducting *design-based research* (DBR), designing is given short shrift, with a great deal of focus put on the designed product and how it instantiates a theory of learning and not on how that type of learning is valued by those it is intended to benefit. This has led some to call into question whether DBR is or involves design (DiSalvo & DiSalvo, 2014).

From the perspective of orthodox design fields (e.g., architecture, engineering, software, fashion) the key activities of designing are well understood and include a focus on the client's needs, framing the problem through empirical work, prototyping potential solutions as a means to better understand the problem/solution space, designing that involves working with constraints, oscillating between problem and solution to optimize the resulting design, and assessing a solution based on how it addresses client needs. Designing—particularly when client needs are sought and the problem and solution are allowed to oscillate—can take on a distinctly emergent, even opportunistic, form, and is typically iterative to the point of being described as *agile* (Beck et al., 2001). Where many in the learning sciences have advanced a stepwise process, those in design fields see their process as involving a much more complex and opportunistic approach. We contend that treating designing as unproblematic limits transferability of our work and holds us back. Being honest about our designing has the potential to aid us—and others—in acquiring insights for and about learning. By, in effect, holding back on what we suggest are authentic aspects of designing, we wonder if we are limiting the new and improved ideas that could benefit the future of education.

In the tradition of worked examples, we present chapters in which authors take this challenge up, laying bare the unlikely sources of inspiration, the design decisions made for better and for worse, detailing twists and turns through itera-tive *and emergent* design processes. Some reveal, perhaps for the first time, that the solution they came up with was not for the problem they started with, and that solution *and problem* co-evolved over the course of their designing (Dorst & Cross, 2001). The chapters highlight designing as a scholarly and worldly act by addressing one or more of these dimensions:

- How needs (both in the world and in our scholarship) were identified
- How constraints were dealt with
- How interdisciplinary design teams were formed and managed
- Where iteration, emergence, or opportunism became important
- To what extent the (worldly and/or scholarly) needs were met.

Of Principles, Patterns, Prototypes, and Getting to Scale

We note there was little agreement on what principles were in the submissions we received for this book. We saw macro and micro principles, descriptive and prescriptive principles. We wonder, are they an externalization of our desire to generalize? Are principles an expectation of funding agencies that then lead to the development of forms of knowledge that become too reified too soon in our design work? In the learning sciences, design principles are treated both as a means to prescribe the instantiation of theory into designed solutions and as a descriptive output of our work as a way to generalize findings. The former appears to stand in for *client needs* when design process is not reported, thus mak-ing it difficult to use these prescriptive principles outside of the original context. Often, this leads to a misfire or malfunction when principles are applied piece-meal or superficially, without sufficient concern for how these principles may function in relationship to the local instructional context.

As a descriptive output of our work, design principles seem to be reported as a matter of course, well in advance of them being observed—across multiple settings—as durable and reliable components of the instructional intervention. When a researcher advances a set of design principles that do not come out of empirical work, but instead from what is believed to be durable knowledge about

learning—often as previously reported in the literature—the resultant principles are *inert*. Such principles are often underspecified in that they do not help guide the implementation of the target intervention *in context*. Without sufficient detail and/or relevance to the design work, the design principles become *look fors* instead of carrying the kind of power that will support innovative practices in new contexts. Those with a positivist point of view expect that design knowledge in the form of principles will have the power to prescribe the procedures for implementing new approaches in real contexts. However, issues with the fidelity of the implementation of new designs argue strongly for the need to allow for local adaptations, and therefore may call for a way of "working with" the principles instead of "working from" the principles.

Similar to fidelity concerns between the quality of CDs and MP3s, the manner in which we compress and communicate educational interventions for the purposes of portability and scaling has resulted in the use of design principles as a means of compressing the essence of learning sciences interventions. However, unlike the success of MP3 files, the results of our attempts to use design principles as a means of moving an intervention to scale still remain to be realized.

William Sandoval (2014) describes the current situation by contrasting embodied conjectures with design principles, which are general, "such as 'make thinking visible.' Such a principle must be interpreted for any particular kind of design to be instantiated. Second, due to their generality, these design principles are unassailable and empirically untestable" (Sandoval, 2014, p. 214). The issue of taking our locally developed designs to scale is perplexing indeed. Early attempts by many in the learning sciences community to maintain the fidelity of the initial instantiation of an educational innovation (Brown, 1992) through adherence to prescriptive design principles has given way to more adaptive approaches to educational improvement. Recently, design-based implementation research (DBIR) has turned this issue around by suggesting that learning sciences researchers interested in effectiveness, relevance, scale, and sustainability should form partnerships with districts such that the design work can come directly from the needs identified by the practitioners and district leaders (Fishman, Penuel, Allen, Cheng, & Sabelli, 2013). However, how existing interventions are to be communicated and thereby adopted by practitioners in the field is an aspect of DBIR that remains to be clarified.

Design patterns are a form of design knowledge that comes from architecture (Alexander et al., 1977) and are intended to serve an intermediary role between theory and practice (Laurillard, 2012). Described as *principled reflective practice*, design patterns are externalized forms of knowledge (Goodyear, 2005) that act as a bridge for teachers in the implementation of an instructional design. Similarly, Bereiter (2014) has proposed *principled practical knowledge (PPK)* as a form of knowledge that is at an intermediary point between theoretical knowledge and practical knowledge. For Bereiter, PPK "provides explanation, but unlike formal theoretical knowledge, its main purpose is not explanation or prediction but

practical guidance" (2014, p. 3). The generation of knowledge of this sort should be a goal of our design work, but too often the knowledge that is developed in the form of principles is too theoretical, too prescriptive, or too abstracted to do the kind of guidance work suggested by Goodyear and Bereiter.

One issue may be our positivist tradition of seeking certainty. A design principle as a *fact* is different than a design principle as a question or proposition. In the early stages of many projects, design principles are identified and stated as facts related to the design. We suggest that design principles based on single-case studies would be better positioned and presented in terms of questions for further exploration. In the design world, this stage of the work would constitute a form of prototyping—the rendering of a solution concept in sufficient detail such that more can be learned about the problem and in turn provide guidance on promising paths to follow with the next iteration. We contend that our scholarship needs to clearly acknowledge that problem framing, which involves doubling back to redefine the problem through projective questioning based on our prototypes, is important and relevant to the advancement of our work. Those in the design fields treat prototyping as primarily an opportunity to learn about the problem/solution space. In many of these chapters the authors reveal how they used their prototypes to learn more about the problem/solution space that then led to further design work.

In contrast, in design fields (e.g., engineering, architecture, fashion), design principles serve to focus on aspects of the design and are generally used consistently across designs. For instance, in fashion design, the designers attend to proportion, balance, unity, and emphasis. Throughout this book we have examples where researchers have struggled both with the difficulty in creating principles to describe what has occurred in their design work and how these principles might be used to instantiate new designs for learning. In particular, as is often the case in the learning sciences, multidisciplinary teams work together to develop these new educational interventions.

Interdisciplinary Collaboration

Design is a fundamentally social and commonly collaborative process (Brereton, Cannon, Mabogunje, & Leifer, 1996; Bucciarelli, 1994; Wood, 2003). As such, it often involves collaboration across disciplines. This can be a source of frustration, but also inspiration. Developing shared understanding can lead to an iterative and even disorganized process (Austin, Steele, Macmillan, Kirby, & Spence, 2001) and can take a great deal of time to establish (Haddon & Kommonen, 2005). Design teams commonly involve those with different sets of expertise (e.g., in learning theory, content areas, technology design, teaching); these groups do not always arrive to the design team valuing each other's sets of expertise (Lingard, Schryer, Spafford, & Campbell, 2007). Each field brings technical language that, when used without explanation, can seem like useless jargon or

can intimidate members and prevent them from making contributions. Likewise, team members arrive with different prior experiences and project expectations. Such differences can create perceived power imbalances that also prevent members from contributing. For instance, when teachers are included on design teams, challenges related to power dynamics can erupt if not managed carefully (Bencze & Hodson, 1999; Hoogveld, Paas, Jochems, & Van Merrienboer, 2002; Penuel & Gallagher, 2009; Reiser et al., 2000). This can mean teachers feel they lack competence and lead to limited participation (diSessa, Azevedo, & Parnafes, 2004). Developing an appreciation of each member's experience and expertise is particularly important for situations in which a possible power imbalance can thwart participation (Kali, Markauskaite, Goodyear, & Ward, 2011). Throughout this book the authors discuss their collaborative activities with team members both in terms of the difficulties encountered with managing and maintaining these relationships and the positive contributions that came from them.

Scholarly and Worldly Client Needs

When designing a device, engineers seek out 'customer needs' as an early means to guide their design work. When designing a research study, education researchers are typically advised to be guided by "theoretical assumptions" (Bogdan & Biklen, 1982), "theoretical orientations" (Mertens, 1998), and the "theoretical drive" (Morse, 2003). As a community, we are adept at locating scholarly needs. Even in DBR, researchers are guided to advance theory, albeit in ways that show "that *context matters* in terms of learning and cognition" (Barab & Squire, 2004, p. 1; emphasis in original); this is accomplished by "learning scientists bring[ing] agendas to their work" (Barab & Squire, 2004, p. 2) in the form of designs for learning.

Learning scientists sometimes bemoan that their designs seldom have a life beyond the research study. We argue that designing for real use includes identifying both scholarly *and* worldly needs, the latter of which deserve a definition. Worldly needs are specific and contextual. Oftentimes, instead of making worldly needs clear, gaps are cited: *minorities are underrepresented in computer science* or *teachers lack tools for making data-informed decisions*. Such gaps may make clear the need for new research, but they do little to shepherd it through myriad decision points involved in designing.

Worldly needs are uncovered by seeking participants' perspectives. Here again, we initially consider this process in engineering. A biomedical engineer designing an artificial limb might seek needs from amputees, but also from doctors or clinicians involved in fitting and monitoring the prosthesis, and even manufacturers. The set of needs would change if the intended market for the prosthesis is amputee athletes or amputees in a rural, isolated community seeking to assemble a prosthesis from items commonly available at a local hardware store.

Context matters in our designing, and seeking worldly needs from participants invites context in. We are less adept at this hard and often time-consuming activity, and further, have few places to detail our efforts to uncover worldly needs.

On occasion, we also do development work, not for others, but for ourselves, identifying our own *felt-needs* and designing based on them. Often, these emerge out of limitations of existing tools—such as tools for conducting analysis—and we seek means to improve upon them. Because we possess an insider view, such designs are likely to appeal to other researchers, as they have similar felt-needs. However, successfully designing for oneself can mislead a designer in how to go about designing for others. Time and effort are needed to understand an unfamiliar context and identify local worldly needs.

As researchers who are also designers, we are tasked with finding ways to balance scholarly and worldly needs. Each design story in this book details how both of these needs were identified. Several design stories also detail how the needs changed over the course of the research, and even how they changed the very course of the research. This nondeterministic, *designerly* approach to research means that not only are we iterative, we are sometimes opportunistic and take advantage of emergent serendipitous situations. We believe it is important that these moves be documented and reported so as a community we have a better appreciation for design in our work.

Opportunism, Emergence, and Iteration

Most introductory research methods courses—and all institutional review boards and ethics committees that review research protocols—emphasize the need to carefully plan each step before conducting a study. We certainly do not argue against the value of planning and a responsibility to protect our research participants. However, when research design is tightly coupled to representations of research predominantly in its final form—that is, traditional published works that have been *sanitized* to mask the designerly complexity of the work we do, this provides not only a poor example of how we do our work, but further, may discourage promising scholars and prevent scholars with promising ideas from pursuing them. These unrealistic portrayals of brilliant science being carried out brilliantly provides little source of inspiration for others to build on.

Design, in the allied design fields, is inherently an emergent, ill-structured problem-solving process. When we design, we find problems and practically solve them to the satisfaction of the client, often with surprising and inspired results. This nondeterministic process is emergent and can often appear opportunistic. If we do not allow design in the learning sciences to function in this manner, we wonder, where will the good ideas come from?

When we asked those in the learning sciences for design stories, many scholars responded with excitement about being able to *admit to being opportunistic.* Even the best-laid plans, it would seem, have been improved on in the process of being carried out. The design stories in this book pull these skeletons out of our closets, providing, we believe, relatable stories that can aid and inspire more designerly actions by learning scientists.

Overview of the Chapters

Each chapter presents a design story. In most cases, the authors have previously published their work in traditional final form elsewhere and reference this. The reader may wish to read those versions in tandem with the design stories presented in this book. We sought chapters that highlighted the *designerly* aspects, process, and decisions that were made. *We take the stance that designing is part of our scholarship*, and as such this message is communicated throughout all the chapters.

D. Kevin O'Neill contributes a design story about the Collaboratory Notebook (O'Neill & Gomez, 1994) software tool. He uses unpublished notes, published papers, and the recollections of the design team to detail decisions made in the design process, specifically, not understanding the context targeted by the design. His story sounds a warning bell for those who aim to design innovative technologies without understanding the context for their use.

Joshua Danish, Noel Enyedy, Asmalina Saleh, and Christine Lee describe how they negotiated context and different scholarly aims as they successfully designed educational technologies for specific elementary science classroom contexts (Danish, 2014; Enyedy, Danish, Delacruz, & Kumar, 2012). They detail how they used activity theory in their design process as a way to carefully attend to context.

Leah Teeters, A. Susan Jurow, and Molly Shea contribute a design story that provides a critical perspective on designing with community members. Through both planful and opportunistic approaches, they navigated barriers common to interdisciplinary teams, and in doing so, developed a scholarly and worldly understanding of the context.

Brian K. Smith writes a design story about Animal Landlord, a video annotation tool/curriculum for high school biology classrooms (Smith & Reiser, 2005). He details the iterative, sometimes serendipitous, design process used and articulates that design is a valuable process in the learning sciences.

Mon-Lin Ko, Susan R. Goldman, and colleagues present a design story in the making, detailing the first 4 years of iterative design-based research focused on instructional designs for argumentation in three disciplines. As a large, interdisciplinary team, they struggled to develop common language, particularly around the design principles they developed to guide their work. They share their design decision making in this process.

Shelley Goldman and Osvaldo Jiménez present the design story of their approach, using a reciprocal research and design process, to creating mobile mathematics applications for families based initially on scholarly needs. They found the design did not function as intended and analyze their successes and failures, presenting the contextual discoveries they uncovered in the process.

Mike Stieff and Stephanie Ryan contribute a design story that recounts the history of the Connected Chemistry Curriculum (CCC) (Levy, Novak, & Wilensky, 2005), a self-contained curriculum and visualization software. They describe the difficult work of understanding constraints, contexts, and learners in their development across multiple classroom implementations. They share some of the relatively mundane aspects that contributed to their success; although a project's success may hang on such details, they are seldom shared in final-form versions of our work.

Palmyre Pierroux and Rolf Steier present a design story that traces the tensions, negotiations, failures, and successes involved in designing a technology in collaboration with a national museum. They detail how scholarly and worldly needs were addressed, as well as how challenges related to interdisciplinary design were navigated. As the project was taken up by others, the goals shifted, leading to new challenges to be navigated.

In assembling these design stories, we selected stories that presented a range of characteristics; they were written by experienced and junior scholars originating from various countries and working on diverse disciplinary topics. Some of the work was completed long ago, and some was in progress at the time the design story was written. Some of the studies aim at small-scale and some at large-scale research. This variability serves to highlight several consistent features of designerly work: (1) forming and maintaining interdisciplinary teams is challenging, yet a rich source for new ideas; (2) locating and respecting worldly needs in tandem with scholarly needs can be time consuming, yet enormously productive; (3) although planning and conducting iterative cycles are important, allowing space for emergence and being opportunistic are common, and even enjoyable, ways to do research; (4) scaling up a design from a small local context can run the risk of transporting a set of principles that—like an armload of differently sized boxes—seem impossible to move from one place to another without dropping some or, at a minimum, rearranging others. We hope these lessons, made salient and vivid in the design stories, contribute to forthright discussions of designing as part of our scholarship.

References

Alexander, C., Ishikawa, S., Silverstein, M., Jacobson, M., Fiksdahl-King, I., & Angel, S. (1977). *A pattern language: Towns, buildings, constructions.* New York, NY: Oxford University Press.

Austin, S., Steele, J., Macmillan, S., Kirby, P., & Spence, R. (2001). Mapping the conceptual design activity of interdisciplinary teams. *Design Studies, 22*(3), 211–232.

Barab, S.A., & Squire, K. (2004). Design-based research: Putting a stake in the ground. *Journal of the Learning Sciences, 13*(1), 1–14. doi:10.1207/s15327809jls1301_1.

Beck, K., Beedle, M., van Bennekum, A., Cockburn, A., Cunningham, W., Fowler, M., . . . Jeffries, R. (2001). The agile manifesto. Retrieved August 3, 2015 from http://www.agilemanifesto.org/.

Bencze, L., & Hodson, D. (1999). Changing practice by changing practice: Toward more authentic science and science curriculum development. *Journal of Research in Science Teaching, 36*(5), 521–539.

Bereiter, C. (2014). Principled practical knowledge: Not a bridge but a ladder. *Journal of the Learning Sciences, 23*(1), 4–17.

Bogdan, R., & Biklen, S. (1982). *Qualitative research for education: An introduction to theory and practice.* New York: Pearson.

Brereton, M.F., Cannon, D.M., Mabogunje, A., & Leifer, L.J. (1996). Collaboration in design teams: How social interaction shapes the product. In N. Cross, H.H.C.M. Christiaans, & K. Dorst (Eds.), *Analysing design activity* (pp. 319–341). Chichester: Wiley.

Brown, A.L. (1992). Design experiments: Theoretical and methodological challenges in creating complex interventions in classroom settings. *The Journal of the Learning Sciences, 2*(2), 141–178. doi:10.1207/s15327809jls0202_2.

Bucciarelli, L.L. (1994). *Designing engineers.* Cambridge, MA: MIT Press.

Danish, J.A. (2014). Applying an activity theory lens to designing instruction for learning about the structure, behavior, and function of a honeybee system. *Journal of the Learning Sciences, 23*(2), 100–148.

DiSalvo, B., & DiSalvo, C. (2014). Designing for democracy in education: Participatory design and the learning sciences. Paper presented at the *11th International Conference of Learning Sciences, ICLS '14*, Boulder, CO.

diSessa, A.A., Azevedo, F.S., & Parnafes, O. (2004). Issues in component computing: A synthetic review. *Interactive Learning Environments, 12*(1–2), 109–159.

Dorst, K., & Cross, N. (2001). Creativity in the design process: Co-evolution of problem-solution. *Design Studies, 22*(5), 425–437.

Enyedy, N., Danish, J.A., Delacruz, G., & Kumar, M. (2012). Learning physics through play in an augmented reality environment. *International Journal of Computer-Supported Collaborative Learning, 7*(3), 347–378.

Fishman, B., Penuel, W.R., Allen, A., Cheng, B.H., & Sabelli, N. (2013). Design-based implementation research: An emerging model for transforming the relationship of research and practice. *National Society for the Study of Education Yearbook, 112*(2), 136–156.

Goodyear, P. (2005). Educational design and networked learning: Patterns, pattern languages and design practice. *Australasian Journal of Educational Technology, 21*(1), 82–101.

Haddon, L., & Kommonen, K.H. (2005). Interdisciplinary explorations: A dialogue between a sociologist and a design group. In L. Haddon (Ed.), *International collaborative research. Cross-cultural differences and cultures of research* (pp. 153–172). COST, Brussels.

Hoogveld, A.W.M., Paas, F., Jochems, W.M.G., & Van Merrienboer, J.J.G. (2002). Exploring teachers' instructional design practices from a systems design perspective. *Instructional Science, 30*(4), 291–305.

Kali, Y., Markauskaite, L., Goodyear, P., & Ward, M.-H. (2011). Bridging multiple expertise in collaborative design for technology-enhanced learning. In H. Spada, G. Stahl, N. Miyake, & N. Law (Eds.), *Proceedings of the Computer Supported Collaborative Learning (CSCL) conference* (pp. 831–835). Hong Kong: International Society of the Learning Sciences.

Laurillard, D. (2012). *Teaching as a design science: Building pedagogical patterns for learning and technology* (pp. 258). New York, NY: Routledge, Taylor & Francis Group.

Levy, S., Novak, M., & Wilensky, U. (2005). *Connected chemistry curriculum 1.3.* Evanston, IL: Center for Connected Learning and Computer Based Modeling, Northwestern University. Retrieved from http://ccl.northwestern.edu/curriculum/ConnectedChemistry/

Lingard, L., Schryer, C.F., Spafford, M.M., & Campbell, S.L. (2007). Negotiating the politics of identity in an interdisciplinary research team. *Qualitative Research, 7*(4), 501–519.

Mertens, D.M. (1998). *Research methods in education and psychology: Integrating diversity with quantitative & qualitative approaches.* Thousand Oaks, CA: Sage Publications.

Morse, J.M. (2003). Principles of mixed methods and multimethod research design. In A. Tashakkori & C. Teddle (Eds.), *Handbook of mixed methods in social and behavioral research,* (pp. 189–208). Thousand Oaks, CA: Sage.

O'Neill, D.K., & Gomez, L.M. (1994). The Collaboratory Notebook: A networked knowledge-building environment for project learning. Paper presented at the *Proceedings of ED-MEDIA 94–World conference on educational multimedia and hypermedia,* Vancouver, British Columbia, Canada.

Penuel, W.R., & Gallagher, L.P. (2009). Preparing teachers to design instruction for deep understanding in middle school Earth science. *Journal of the Learning Sciences, 18*(4), 461–508.

Reiser, B.J., Spillane, J.P., Steinmuller, F., Sorsa, D., Carney, K., & Kyza, E. (2000). Investigating the mutual adaptation process in teachers' design of technology-infused curricula. In B. Fishman & S. O'Connor-Divelbiss (Eds.), *Proceedings of the fourth international conference of the learning sciences* (pp. 342–349). Mahwah, NJ: Erlbaum.

Sandoval, W. (2014). Conjecture mapping: An approach to systematic educational design research. *Journal of the Learning Sciences, 23*(1), 18–36. doi:10.1080/10508406.2013.77 8204.

Smith, B.K., & Reiser, B.J. (2005). Explaining behavior through observational investigation and theory articulation. *Journal of the Learning Sciences, 14*(3), 315–360. doi:10. 1207/s15327809jls1403_1.

Wood, W.H. (2003). Integrating social issues into design theory. *International Journal of Engineering Education, 19*(1), 35–40.

2

DESIGNING THE COLLABORATORY NOTEBOOK

"Building the Future, the Night Before It's Due"

D. Kevin O'Neill

One science only will one genius fit:
So vast is art, so narrow human wit:
Not only bounded to peculiar arts,
But oft in those confined to single parts.
Like kings we lose the conquests gain'd before,
By vain ambition still to make them more:
Each might his servile province well command,
Would all but stoop to what they understand.

Alexander Pope (1711, p. 6)

Introduction

The Collaboratory Notebook (Edelson, Pea, & Gomez, 1996; O'Neill & Gomez, 1994) is a computer-supported collaborative learning tool that is now more than 20 years old. It cannot run on any computer made today, but the story of its development still offers learning scientists valuable lessons about the design work they do now and the pitfalls that lie in their path.

I helped to create the Collaboratory Notebook at Northwestern University as part of the National Science Foundation (NSF)–funded *Learning Through Collaborative Visualization* (CoVis) project (Pea, 1993), a multimillion-dollar effort started in 1992 to explore the potential of wide-area networking technologies (i.e., broadband Internet) to enable project-based science teaching in US high schools. One of several funded "school network testbeds," the special focus of CoVis was on project-based teaching that would make use of current weather and climate data, data visualization tools, and direct collaboration between students and scientists.

CoVis started with two Chicago-area high schools, each of which got high-speed Internet access and a specially outfitted classroom containing six high-end Macintosh workstations and six desktop videoconferencing systems. Through these workstations, six teachers and their students would have access not only to reference materials, scientific data, and data visualization tools, but also to *people* with deep scientific expertise, including atmospheric scientists at the University of Illinois at Urbana–Champaign and "explainers" at the Exploratorium in San Francisco.

From my perspective, the CoVis vision was that students would *have* to have a way to keep track of the data they used on their workstations and how they interpreted it, so they could undertake challenging, long-term investigations and share them with their project partners, teachers, and distant experts. The Collaboratory Notebook was intended to address this need. When the work began, I was a freshly minted computer science B.Sc. and first-year student in a new Ph.D. program called "Learning Sciences." Danny Edelson, a research scientist with a Ph.D. in computer science, led the effort. He also managed a full-time programmer, Joey Gray, who brought years of industry experience to our work. Two CoVis principal investigators (PIs), Roy Pea and Louis Gomez, regularly reviewed our work and probed us with critical questions. Other graduate students on the CoVis team provided valuable input into the design as well.

The Collaboratory Notebook was an impressive technological achievement for its time. In 1992 when we started work on this software, the first graphical web browser (NCSA Mosaic) had not yet been released. Most of the general public had not even heard of the Internet, much less used it. They wouldn't have *wanted* to use it then—it was a pretty unpleasant experience. Most people who used e-mail (then a small fraction of the population) did so through purely text-based terminal programs. Friendly dial-up gateway services such as America Online were just getting started. So, a usable piece of software designed specifically for doing collaborative science projects was a bold and novel undertaking.

Using the Collaboratory Notebook software, individual students were able to create and co-author electronic "notebooks" to document science projects (see Figure 2.1).

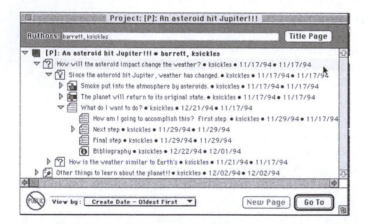

FIGURE 2.1   A notebook table of contents

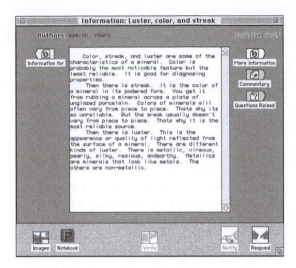

FIGURE 2.2 A notebook page in "reading" view

A notebook could have just one author, or several, and these authors could all access and add to the notebook simultaneously from any Macintosh connected to the Internet (a Windows client was created later). Notebooks contained "pages" made up of plain text, though images and files could be attached to each page. Pages could be linked to one another, and each page could have multiple authors (see Figure 2.2). This meant that if they wanted to, a large group (such as a class or parts of different classes) could share one notebook for an ongoing project, and particular groups of students could co-author individual pages within it.

Academically, the Collaboratory Notebook software had a substantial impact, with some publications accumulating over 100 citations, but this is not what makes the software interesting to think about in the context of this book. It is important to note that the most highly cited papers about the Collaboratory Notebook were "vision" pieces that discussed the potential that we—the software's co-creators—saw in it and that shared carefully chosen examples of use that we aligned with our vision. There were relatively few empirical papers that described what larger numbers of people were doing with the software, partly because so few people used the system.

Focal Design Process Elements

In what follows, I will tell my version of the story of the Collaboratory Notebook as I have often used it in teaching over the years: as a parable about how *not* to go about designing technology for schools. There is more than one way to tell this story, and I will make an effort to acknowledge other perspectives on these events. In the view that I will present, however, one of the main problems

I see with our design process was that we did not invest enough of the right kinds of effort in needs assessment (or in software terms, requirements analysis) with the students and teachers we aimed to serve. As a result, the design that evolved stressed the scholarly needs of the designers over the practical needs of the teachers and students we were designing for. My main goal here is to explain how—despite being well resourced and well motivated to serve the needs of our initial target audience of six teachers, we provided a tool in which most of them took little interest.

Developing such an explanation requires looking at how the context in which the software was created shaped a particular design "frame" (Dorst, 2011)—a set of assumptions about what the Collaboratory Notebook should be, what it needed to do, and how the design work should be conducted. Many of the pressures that shaped this frame are still at work today. In the discussion, I will use the Collaboratory Notebook story to illustrate two potential "traps" that I believe still endanger learning scientists' design work and offer suggestions about how to avoid them.

Design Story

The reader will appreciate that it is challenging to write an account of a design process so long after the fact. To further complicate matters, none of the members of the Collaboratory Notebook design team (myself included) were particularly concerned about capturing our design process. This fact is fairly ironic in my case. Once, in a CoVis meeting, someone asked what data we should be collecting that we weren't already collecting. I suggested that we should imagine ourselves 10 years in the future, trying to write the history of CoVis, and let that be our guide. This response garnered some quizzical looks, but here I am spinning a CoVis yarn more than 20 years later.

Published work about the Collaboratory Notebook is mute about our design process; thus, to supplement the published record, I have had to rely on several folders of paper notes that I held onto over the years. These folders contain lengthy written arguments by various CoVis team members about why a particular design direction should be taken or not, hastily drawn sketches documenting suggestions about how part of the interface might look and work (e.g. Figure 2.3), handwritten summaries of meetings in which design decisions were made, and documentation written for the teachers we hoped would use the software. Some of the documents are formally written and dated; others are casually written and undated, clearly not intended for posterity.

These are like the sources any historian would typically work with and present similar challenges of interpretation. With this evidence, it is unfortunately not possible to reconstruct our design process in a clear and precise way. However, Danny Edelson agreed to be interviewed specifically for this chapter late in 2014 and helped fill in gaps and inform my interpretations. He has also read and

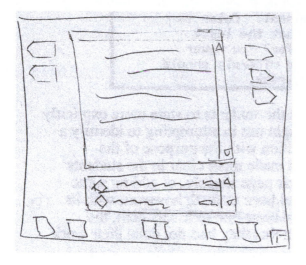

FIGURE 2.3 An early design sketch

provided generous feedback on drafts of this chapter, though what I offer here is my own personal view of our experience.

In an important sense, the design of the Collaboratory Notebook began with its name, which was written into the original CoVis grant proposal. The principal investigators on that grant, Roy Pea, Louis Gomez, and Elliot Soloway, had been inspired by an NSF report on networked scientific laboratories ("collaboratories," Lederberg & Uncapher, 1989). The name they chose for our software, "Collaboratory Notebook," married this inspiring concept of a collaborative laboratory with the familiar concept of a science student's laboratory notebook. The name provided the main organizing metaphor for the software's design, which stuck with it throughout its lifecycle. It also distinguished the design from other systems, such as the earlier CSILE (Computer Support Intentional Learning Environment—later Knowledge Forum; Scardamalia, Bereiter, McLean, Swallow, & Woodruff, 1989), which was based on the metaphor of a communal classroom database of knowledge. Rather than defaulting to a single, classroom-wide knowledge base, in the Collaboratory Notebook, notebooks (like physical ones) were thought of as personal and private by default.

The design team's work started from three key assumptions:

1. CoVis students would do science projects in groups.
2. Students would need some way to document their thinking and work with scientific data drawn from the Internet so that their collaborators could access it and their teachers could review, provide guidance on, and grade it.
3. To make the most of CoVis institutional partners and volunteer scientists, students' work had to be accessible at a distance over the Internet.

This is not an extensive set of assumptions on which to design a complex new software system. Indeed, we made quite a few more assumptions. How did the design team arrive at these assumptions? My notes and recollections suggest that, for the most part, we decided on these ourselves. As far as I recall, we never brought the prospective users in to discuss what they wanted, and we never showed them mockups of our ideas before writing code. Instead, we pursued the design of the software by arguing about our prospective users' needs in their absence.

It would be a mistake to suggest that we didn't care about the students and teachers for whom we were building the Collaboratory Notebook. We did, but we did not seriously investigate what their needs were. What is especially surprising about us *not* engaging teachers and students in the design process is that the CoVis team had a rare advantage that could have enabled such engagement. Pea, Gomez, and Soloway had wisely proposed a funded planning year for CoVis, which included release time for the original six teachers. The teachers each got time off from work to read about and discuss project pedagogy together and met regularly with the whole CoVis team to prepare for the first implementation year. I attended many of these meetings. So, why did we not involve the teachers in crafting the software at this stage? I can think of three reasons.

First, like many other would-be reformers, we were in a terrible hurry (Bryk, Gomez, Grunow, & LeMahieu, 2015). The initial CoVis grant was for 3 years. Part of the initial planning year was consumed with putting staff in place to start work on the software. This schedule didn't leave much time to develop a new, complex system from the ground up and put it in students' hands by the start of year two. We believed the Collaboratory Notebook software was essential for students and teachers to get the most value out of the rest of the expensive technology they were to be given, so we rushed to get a working system ready for the start of CoVis' first classroom implementation year. A fellow Northwestern graduate student (and author of another chapter in this volume), Brian Smith, observed some of the CoVis graduate students working late nights and invented the wry slogan, "Learning Sciences: building the future, the night before it's due!"

The second reason we didn't choose to involve our prospective users in the design work was that, in our view, they did not know much about this kind of technology. They were smart, and they were computer users, but in the early days of the project we were literally teaching them how to use e-mail and explaining what a server was. Add to this the fact that, despite their backgrounds in computer science, the design team had no real experience in conducting a software requirements analysis—a process that remains poorly understood by many software developers (Lauesen, 2002; Nuseibeh & Easterbrook, 2000; Urquhart, 1998). Thus, we simply couldn't conceive *how* to meaningfully involve the teachers in shaping the design of something so unlike anything they had ever used.

Third—and most crucial, in my view—in addition to agreeing that the CoVis teachers did not know enough about software to take part in the design work, I suspect we convinced ourselves that they didn't know enough about the amazing future of project-based science teaching either. In retrospect, I admit this view seems condescending; recall that in 1992, CoVis brought together high-speed Internet, full-screen video conferencing, and a strong group of institutional partners with deep scientific expertise in order to *reform* high school science education. All this, combined with the schedule pressure, I believe made it easy for us to convince ourselves that we were inventing the *future* and should not be beholden to *current* practices.

So, if you're building software to support teaching and don't feel beholden to current teaching practices, where do you find the design inspiration you need?

Pivotal Design Choices

Being aspiring academics, we looked to the literature to inform design choices that we expected to publish articles on later. In this way, *our* needs as designers began to take priority in framing the design problem. One apparently fateful set of choices made by the team was driven by our cognitive science orientation to learning, which stressed making expert cognitive processes explicit for novices (Bransford, Brown, & Cocking, 2000). Based on research introduced to us at the time, we felt it would be ideal for the online notebooks produced by students to scaffold their inquiry through the design of the interface itself. A unique approach to this problem was the key innovation we decided to embody in the software.

The basic approach of including scaffolding in software was not unique: CSILE/Knowledge Forum (Scardamalia & Bereiter, 1994; Scardamalia et al., 1989), Inquire (Brunner, 1990), and other systems of that era involved procedural supports or "thinking types" as well. These were often justified by referring to Edward de Bono (de Bono, 1985), Stephen Toulmin (Toulmin, 1958), and other famous scholars. Designers of collaborative systems in that day would engage in lengthy arguments about the relative merits of one set of hypertext node and link types over another—as I experienced firsthand in 1994 at the Computer-Supported Collaborative Work conference (O'Neill, Gomez, & Edelson, 1994).

Understanding the need to keep the Collaboratory Notebook's interface simple for our users—and wanting to keep things simple for ourselves as well—we designed our notebook page-writing interface in such a way that each page could have just one "type" assigned to it. The page types, which were intended to reflect norms of scientific argument but were not explicitly based on any particular theory, included question, plan, conjecture, evidence for, evidence against, commentary, and information. They had cute icons (see Figure 2.4), and to make sure that students didn't forget to pick one, the system simply refused to save their work until they did.

One of the Collaboratory Notebook's most distinctive features, however, was a restrictive grammar that dictated how pages of various types could be linked

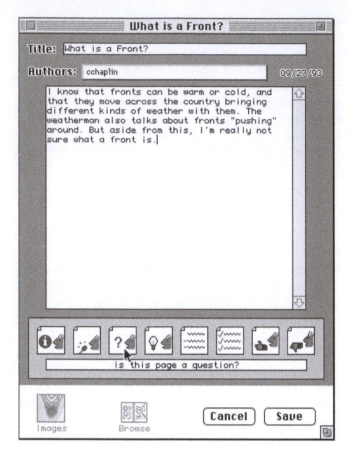

FIGURE 2.4 A notebook page in "writing" view, with page type picker at the bottom

together (see Figure 2.5). For example, students weren't allowed to save a page labeled a "step in a plan" before first saving a page labeled "plan." The software made it valid to respond to a question with a conjecture, or to a conjecture with a question, but *not* to respond to a commentary with a conjecture. We described this page grammar as a way of scaffolding students' scientific thinking, though in retrospect I suspect students more often felt frustrated or confused by it than supported. Many users didn't understand why the palette of allowed response types changed from page to page, and no overview of the linking grammar was available in the software itself—only in the teacher manual.

In hindsight, from my perspective, the problem with our design wasn't that we asked students to tag their work with thinking types, but that we forced them to break up their ideas on different pages, label each one in order to save it, and save thoughts of different kinds in a particular order. Although I feel a pang of guilt in writing about these design choices today, my experience at Computer-Supported

Nov. 17, 1993

Response Scaffolding

Page Type	Response Pallette	
Information	Information,	Question
	Commentary	
Question	Information,	Question
	Commentary	
	Conjecture	Plan
Commentary	Information,	Question
	Commentary	
Conjecture	Information,	Question
	Commentary,	
	Conjecture	Plans,
	Evidence For	Evidence Against
Plan	Information,	Question
	Commentary,	
	Step in a Plan	
Step in a Plan	Information,	Question
	Commentary	
Evidence For	Information,	Question
	Commentary	
Evidence Against	Information,	Question
	Commentary	

FIGURE 2.5   The Collaboratory Notebook page grammar (from 1993 documentation)

Cooperative Work conferences in 1994 and 1998 suggests that similarly overt ways of shaping peoples' thinking and workflow in the design of collaborative media were rampant at the time.

Initial Response from Users

The original six CoVis teachers encountered the Collaboratory Notebook for the first time at a summer workshop in 1993 as a fully functioning, if somewhat raw, software system (the cute icons hadn't been designed yet). Some teachers were slightly more enthusiastic than others, but it is fair to say that their reactions were

Part of the reason we designed the Collaboratory Notebook with page types and a restrictive page-linking grammar was that we had framed the project as a piece of research in its own right. Because we thought of the software design as research, it didn't seem sufficient to simply provide an open space for students to save words and data where remote collaborators could access them and link them in any way they wanted to. We assumed that to support innovation, the software itself had to contain innovative features. However, our efforts could have been framed in other ways. In retrospect, we *could* have framed the Collaboratory Notebook in our minds as a piece of *infrastructure* to support the larger CoVis research agenda. If we had done so, we would have felt less pressure to include "innovative" features in the software that reduced its flexibility. We could instead have looked for innovative practices to emerge from students' and teachers' behavior around and through the software. As we recognized these practices inductively, we could have incorporated new features into the system to facilitate them. Naturally, this inductive approach would have taken more time; we would only have been able to begin the process under the initial 3-year grant, and might not have gotten the chance to go further.

Trap #1: Building the Future

This brings me to the first trap we fell into, which lies in wait for scholar-designers today. We live in an age in which most people share a faith that our future will be continuously redefined by computing technology. Indeed, this faith motivates many of the people who enter our field, as well as those who invest money in our work. Unfortunately, the faith in the power of new ideas and technologies to reshape social practice also makes learning scientists vulnerable to a naïve grandiosity that my story of the Collaboratory Notebook illustrates well. To put it bluntly, we may expect our inventions to reshape social practice to a far greater degree than they can and far more rapidly than they can. This grandiosity is not unique to information technology designers, which is why Pope described it so well in the 1700s.

The fact that none of the members of the core design team for the Collaboratory Notebook had ever taught in a K–12 school might have inspired us to do careful needs analysis with teachers and students. Instead, under the schedule pressure, we convinced ourselves that these needs could not be empirically examined because the teaching practices we aimed to support would necessarily be different from those of the present. At the time, we said and believed, "We're not building software to support how they teach today. We're building software to support how they will teach in the future." In retrospect I view this belief as convenient, but sadly mistaken.

Given the commonness of computer-supported collaborative learning (CSCL) tools today and students' and teachers' increasing comfort with them, it is possible to argue that the Collaboratory Notebook was ahead of its time, but such an argument misses the point. A designed artifact of any kind needs to be useful in its *own* time and support *existing* practices, at least to some degree. Without a careful examination of existing practices, such as the examination of cultural practices that informed Lee's successful use of a modified version of the Collaboratory Notebook, most attempts to "build the future" are doomed to fail. Years after the initial design work on the Collaboratory Notebook, I realize that the world of practice is simply too complex and intricate for us to hope to strike it lucky without doing our homework.

Trap #2: Desperation for Success

The second trap that lies in wait for learning scientists is more subtle. It is unavoidably the case with university-based design research that the work requires the investment of a large amount of time on the part of young people who, not coincidentally, are attempting to build careers. Members of any team like ours would realize it would not serve their interests to be associated with an expensive failure; I think, quite naturally, we tried not to think of our work as such. I do not mean to suggest that we were engaged in cynical self-promotion, but subtle forms of self-interest and prejudice have been blinding to scientists throughout history (Gould, 1981).

Resistance to admitting failure had particular consequences in our case. Facing a target audience that didn't like what we had built, it was easier to search out other, more appreciative audiences than tear our finely crafted edifice down and build it again. Also, because we had to publish and knew that reviewers favor successes over failures, we did our best to find success in what we had done. This led to some of the least-referenced papers to emerge from CoVis (e.g., O'Neill, Edelson, Gomez, & D'Amico, 1995). I wish I could tell you that I thought we were alone in the desperation we felt when writing these papers, but decades of experience in reviewing journal submissions tells me otherwise.

As I mentioned earlier, the Collaboratory Notebook design team believed that by embodying our ideas in software and putting that software out in the world for people to use, we were testing a theory. Unfortunately, as framed, the only disconfirming evidence that it was possible for us to find for our theory was people simply not using the software. In our desperation to find success, we explained the lack of use away with reference to a slow network, computers with too little memory, and teachers who were not prepared for what we believed was to be the inevitable future. In this way, we could avoid facing the possibility that the Collaboratory Notebook's most distinctive design features were flawed.

Avoiding the Traps

Now that I've described the traps, what, if anything, can be done to avoid them?

Avoiding the trap of "building the future" is challenging because at the present time, the culture that surrounds us seems to encourage grandiose technological visions and to disregard history. Swimming against the stream is always hard, but the most effective remedy I can think of for this problem is stories like the one you're reading, which demonstrate how visionary futurist design, uninformed by current practice, can go wrong. Stories, in whatever medium, can have enormous instructional power (Schank, 1990), and I hope that reading this one can save other scholar-designers some anguish.

Avoiding the trap of desperation for success is more difficult. Although it is undeniably important for learning scientists to try out bold new designs like the Collaboratory Notebook, for these efforts to be useful *as scholarship*, we need to be equally willing to abandon them and report their failure in a way that did not seem possible in the present case. I've argued before that our field needs to develop a new connoisseurship of informative failed designs (O'Neill, 2012) so that there are incentives for learning scientists to report design failures well—and in a far more timely way than I am demonstrating here!

Public sharing of failure is one of the key ways in which a very successful design science—aeronautics—actually progressed from hops of a few seconds to flights of 30 minutes and more in the early 1900s. In Paris in that day, aircraft designers used a French military parade ground called *Issy les Moulineaux* as their airfield for testing. All of their (mostly unsuccessful) tests were carried out in full view of whoever chose to show up. This openness meant that the failures informed everyone, and when the first promising designs were hit upon, they spread rapidly too (Vincenti, 1990).

One of the best ways I can imagine to create an openness to reporting design failures in the learning sciences is to establish a norm that senior scholars publish such failures together with the junior scholars who help to develop them. For the record, I do not recall ever being discouraged from reporting what I perceived to be the failures of the Collaboratory Notebook. I censored myself. The challenge that stands before us today is to make it possible for junior scholars not to feel it necessary to censor themselves in this way. Establishing new scholarly norms has historically been a lengthy process (Bazerman, 1988), but as the story of the Collaboratory Notebook underscores, we can't be in a rush about creating worthwhile change. I hope that this design story can serve as a beginning for such change.

References

Bazerman, C. (1988). *Shaping written knowledge: The genre and activity of the experimental article in science.* Madison, WI: University of Wisconsin Press.

Bransford, J.D., Brown, A.L., & Cocking, R.R. (2000). *How people learn: Brain, mind, experience, and school* (expanded ed.). Washington, DC: National Academy Press.

Brunner, C. (1990). *Designing inquire* (Technical Report No. 50). New York: Center for Children and Technology, Bank Street College of Education.

Bryk, A.S., Gomez, L.M., Grunow, A., & LeMahieu, P.G. (2015). *Learning to improve: How America's schools can get better at getting better.* Cambridge, MA: Harvard Education Press.

de Bono, E. (1985). *Six thinking hats.* Boston, MA: Little, Brown.

Dorst, K. (2011). The core of 'design thinking' and its application. *Design Studies, 32*(6), 521–532.

Edelson, D.C., Pea, R., & Gomez, L.M. (1996). The Collaboratory Notebook. *Communications of the ACM, 39*(4), 32–33.

Gould, S.J. (1981). *The mismeasure of man.* New York, NY: Norton.

Kyza, E.A., & Edelson, D.C. (2005). Scaffolding middle-school students' coordination of theory and evidence. *Educational Research and Evaluation, 11*(6), 545–560.

Lauesen, S. (2002). *Software requirements: Styles and techniques.* London: Addison-Wesley.

Lederberg, J., & Uncapher, K. (March 17–18, 1989). Towards a national collaboratory: Report of an invitational workshop at the Rockefeller University. Washington, DC: National Science Foundation Directorate for Computer and Information Science.

Lee, C.D. (2003). Toward a framework for culturally responsive design in multimedia computer environments: Cultural modeling as a case. *Mind, Culture and Activity, 10*(1), 42–61.

Nuseibeh, B., & Easterbrook, S. (2000). Requirements engineering: A roadmap. Paper presented at the *ACM Conference on software engineering,* Limerick, Ireland.

O'Neill, D.K. (2012). Designs that fly: What the history of aeronautics tells us about the future of design-based research in education. *International Journal of Research & Method in Education, 35*(2), 119–140.

O'Neill, D.K., Edelson, D.C., Gomez, L.M., & D'Amico, L.M. (1995). *Learning to weave collaborative hypermedia into classroom practice.* Paper presented at CSCL '95: Computer Support for Collaborative Learning, Indiana University, Bloomington.

O'Neill, D.K., & Gomez, L.M. (1994). The Collaboratory Notebook: A networked knowledge-building environment for project learning. Paper presented at the *Proceedings of ED-MEDIA 94–World conference on educational multimedia and hypermedia,* Vancouver, British Columbia, Canada.

O'Neill, D.K., Gomez, L.M., & Edelson, D.C. (1994). Collaborative hypermedia for the classroom and beyond: A year's experiences with the Collaboratory Notebook. Paper presented at the CSCW '94: *Workshop on collaborative hypermedia systems,* Chapel Hill, North Carolina.

Pea, R.D. (1993). Distributed multimedia learning environments: The collaborative visualization project. *Communications of the ACM, 36*(5), 60–63.

Pope, A. (1711). *An essay on criticism.* Yorkshire, England: Scolar Press.

Scardamalia, M., & Bereiter, C. (1994). Computer support for knowledge-building communities. *Journal of the Learning Sciences, 3*(3), 265–283.

Scardamalia, M., Bereiter, C., McLean, R.S., Swallow, J., & Woodruff, E. (1989). Computer-supported intentional learning environments. *Educational Computing Research, 5*(1), 51–68.

Schank, R.C. (1990). *Tell me a story: A new look at real and artificial memory.* New York, NY: Charles Scribner's Sons.

Toulmin, S. (1958). *The uses of argument.* Cambridge, UK: Cambridge University Press.

Urquhart, C. (1998). Analysts and clients in conversation: Cases in early requirements gathering. Paper presented at the *ICIS '98: Proceedings of the international conference on Information systems,* Helsinki, Finland.

Vincenti, W.G. (1990). *What engineers know and how they know it: Analytical studies from aeronautical history.* Baltimore, MD: The Johns Hopkins University Press.

3

DESIGNING FOR ACTIVITY

*Joshua Danish, Noel Enyedy, Asmalina Saleh,
and Christine Lee*

Introduction

In this chapter, we describe our efforts to use activity theory (Engeström, 1987) as a framework for the design of new educational technologies and activities. Activity theory is one of the general classes of theories that are commonly labeled "sociocultural" for their focus on the relationship between learning and rich cultural contexts (John-Steiner & Mahn, 1996). The promise of activity theory for supporting educational design efforts lies in its potential for systematically articulating the relationship between the intended goals of the design, the features of the technology, and the sociocultural context in which it will be realized (Kaptelinin & Nardi, 2006; Nardi, 1996), enabling understanding of why things worked or failed in hindsight. However, a common critique of sociocultural theories is that for prospective design, they often require designers to attend to *too many* elements at once. This can lead to designers either becoming lost in a quagmire of possibilities or *guessing* in unsystematic ways that no longer benefit from the structure provided by theory, and the result is that design decisions are effectively arbitrary and difficult to evaluate or explain (Witte & Haas, 2005). We share how we have productively structured our own activity theory designs to move beyond this quagmire in a theoretically grounded manner.

We contrast two projects: BeeSign and Learning Physics through Play (LPP). BeeSign (Danish, 2014; Danish, Peppler, Phelps, & Washington, 2011) is a software tool and series of activities designed to help kindergarten and first-grade students explore complex systems concepts in the context of honeybees collecting nectar. The LPP project is a mixed-reality environment designed to help first- and second-grade students learn the basic concepts of force and motion (Enyedy, Danish, Delacruz, & Kumar, 2012; Enyedy, Danish, & DeLiema, 2015).

We contrast these two projects because they were designed and implemented in a similar context (the same elementary school), and yet we found it necessary to choose different solutions when faced with similar challenges.

Designing with Activity Theory

Although activity theory has many elements, there are two interrelated principles that drive our design efforts—the notion of social mediation and the idea of learning as appropriation (John-Steiner & Mahn, 1996). *Mediation* refers to the idea that there are always cultural artifacts that *lie between* an individual and the object of his or her activity. The object of activity refers to both the goals that someone is pursuing and the physical objects with which he or she is interacting. Cultural artifacts refer to physical tools—such as computer simulations—and conceptual tools—such as ideas about force and motion. Cultural artifacts such as these transform how we see and engage with the world. So, in our examples, a computer simulation fundamentally alters the experience students have with the behavior of honeybees or the laws of physics.

Closely related to mediation is the concept of *appropriation*. Appropriation refers to the idea that all learning begins when we encounter ideas within the social world (Vygotsky, 1978). Individuals then transform these ideas as they internalize them by re-creating them in their mind. We use this in our designs by assuming students will encounter new concepts or practices *within the social interactions that we design*. We also assume that students will appropriate them in idiosyncratic ways, and thus we aim to support opportunities for them to continually articulate and refine their understanding.

Focal Design Elements

In our design efforts, we pay careful attention to how the software and activities we design will mediate students' activity systems in ways that will promote appropriation of the target concepts. This necessarily involves a consideration of the existing activity system and the entire range of possible mediators. In attempting to identify existing activities and mediators, we first encounter the challenge that activity theory brings with it: How much of the activity system should we attend to and how can we identify the key elements? Other theorists have suggested a number of ways to address this dilemma, including asking a lengthy battery of questions about the environment (Mwanza-Simwami, 2013).

We have found that a valuable first step is to observe the collaborating classrooms and begin to identify key mediators and activity structures. Similar to the process of participatory design (Carroll & Rosson, 2007), which is well aligned with activity theory (Bødker, 2009), we assume that the future users of our designs will have a great deal of explicit and tacit knowledge that shape how the designs are taken up. Therefore, we try to join the classroom as participants, allowing us to better appreciate what the mediators are and how they transform the work of the classroom community. A key step in this process is to work collaboratively with our partners to vet our understanding of the classroom practices and solicit feedback as we iteratively refine our design ideas (Spinuzzi, 2005). This allows us to tap into teacher expertise while being cognizant of how the design is affecting teachers and students, as well as providing the teachers with some ownership of the design process (Carroll & Rosson, 2007). From a participatory design perspective, our implementation within the classroom is also more akin to a prototyping process (Bødker, 2009; Spinuzzi, 2005) than a final-form design; our goal is to continually refine our designs as we explore their utility in the local classroom as part of an ongoing design experiment (Brown, 1992) that aims to understand how and why our designs work rather than simply demonstrating that they do.

Our goal is not to identify *all* of the mediators that exist, but to focus on those that we believe are likely to affect our ongoing design efforts. We then refine this focus through discussion and early design efforts. For example, we initially noted that teachers used their time at the rug for whole-class discussions. Upon further reflection, we realized that rug time served two roles of interest to our work: introducing new ideas for the whole group and helping to summarize ideas that different subgroups of students encountered so that their peers could benefit from their realizations.

Initial Exploration: Observing the School

We began our process in a manner similar to the exploratory stage described in the participatory design literature, attempting to familiarize ourselves with the existing classroom culture with a focus on how users function within the local space (Spinuzzi, 2005). To this end, Danish and Enyedy began participating in the classrooms that would later host BeeSign and LPP as early as 2003, working as participant observers and collecting data for other research projects that were not design oriented (c.f., Danish & Enyedy, 2007). Inspired by the idea of anthropological activism (Papert, 1993)—studying a cultural system and then attempting to affect change from within the system as a participant—our aim is to understand the cultural context of the classroom as much as possible before we attempt to work with teachers to transform it. To develop BeeSign (and later LPP), we began by identifying the existing high-level organizing structures in the classroom, focusing on those that appear to be central to how the teachers support student learning. We believe that we are more likely to reap the benefits of working with experienced professionals if we can integrate our own designs into structures that are already familiar to teachers and students. For example, we identified rug time and stations in our classroom—both of which are quite common in early elementary classrooms. Stations refer to physical spaces that are organized within the larger classroom. Groups of students move between stations as they work together on activities that occur in parallel. We built our activities around the use of both rug time and stations in order to effectively integrate them in the existing classroom dynamics.

Stuck in the Quagmire: Tensions between Conceptual and Social Goals

Our early classroom observations highlighted an immediate dilemma between our cognitive or conceptual goals and the social goals and constraints of the space.

At the *cognitive and conceptual level*, educational designers often think of the sequence in which students will explore the content. Typically, we think of students as moving from simple ideas to more complex ideas, though the literature also notes the value of experiential sequences such as moving from the concrete to the abstract. This goal of designing around a sequence appeared to be at direct odds with the *social and cultural reality* of our target classroom. The use of stations provided a context in which students were necessarily viewing different aspects of the content in parallel. This was further complicated by a very real logistical issue: even in a well-resourced classroom with teachers' aides, the amount of support that students could receive at each station was variable as the teachers aimed to provide assistance where it was most needed. Therefore, we began our design efforts keenly aware of this tension between typical treatment of content in a sequential manner and the practical organization of the classroom around small-group work interspersed with occasional whole-class discussions at the rug. Although we feel activity theory helped us identify this tension, it does not immediately suggest a single path forward. We present how the two projects explored this tension and the dilemmas that arose.

Design Story #1 BeeSign: Designed to Support Complex Systems Understanding

Impetus

The idea for BeeSign emerged from our work in exploring how students created science representations in our collaborating classroom (Danish & Enyedy, 2007). In this earlier study, we observed students' approach to creating representations within their existing science curriculum, which happened to include plant biology and pollination. We realized that when representing pollination, the students engaged in particularly rich and productive discussions and appeared to be exhibiting complex systems thinking—an awareness of how multiple organisms (pollinators and flowers) interrelate in powerful ways that are not easily explained by observing any single element on its own. Although this kind of reasoning is considered incredibly powerful across disciplines (NRC, 2012), the inherent difficulty of the content has led researchers to focus primarily upon older students, providing us with an exciting opportunity to research how younger students might engage productively with these concepts. We decided to focus more narrowly on honeybees collecting nectar as a context that is both familiar to students and touches on complex systems concepts.

Conceptual Goals and Design

Complex systems are collections of interdependent and interrelated elements whose properties emerge from their interactions, often in nonintuitive ways. One of the challenges of learning about systems is that students often have to view them from multiple levels simultaneously. For example, Hmelo-Silver, Marathe, and Liu (2007) have noted that systems might be viewed in terms of *structures* such as the proboscis (tongue) that the bees use to collect nectar, *behaviors* such as the "waggle dance" that bees use to communicate the location of a source of nectar to other bees in the hive, and a *function* of this waggle in helping the hive as a whole collect nectar efficiently (see Danish, 2014).

Using Activity Theory to Narrow the Field of Possibilities

Having identified some key structures, behaviors, and functions of the honeybee system, we returned to the dilemma of how to address these productively within the collaborating classroom. How might we engage students with these multiple perspectives? How can activity theory help us productively identify the best set of activities in which to do this? In mere moments of brainstorming, hundreds of possible activities emerged, but how to choose between them and refine them productively? Our next step was to explore the key "activities" from an activity theory perspective.

Although the term "activity" has many colloquial connotations, activity theorists use this term to refer to collective, object-oriented activity, which is viewed as the primary unit of analysis for understanding cognition and learning (Engeström, 1987). The defining characteristic of activity is, therefore, an object (or overarching goal) that is shared by the participants. Activity theory then defines the mediators such as tools, rules, and the division of labor, which help transform an individual's participation in the activity as he or she pursues the object. This relationship is often represented as an activity triangle (see Figure 3.1). All of these mediators are presumed to be interrelated, challenging the activity theorist to think about how the relationships support students in pursuing their joint object.

This collection of rich interrelations is what has led critics to suggest that activity theory is challenging to apply (Witte & Haas, 2005). However, we view this as a strength of activity theory and have developed a heuristic approach to covering this space: 1) identify the object, 2) focus on appropriation, 3) identify

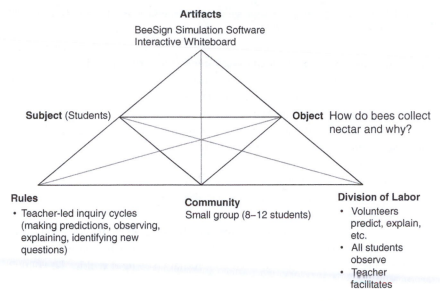

Artifacts
BeeSign Simulation Software
Interactive Whiteboard

Subject (Students)

Object How do bees collect
nectar and why?

Rules
• Teacher-led inquiry cycles
  (making predictions, observing,
  explaining, identifying new
  questions)

Community
Small group (8–12 students)

Division of Labor
• Volunteers
  predict, explain,
  etc.
• All students
  observe
• Teacher
  facilitates

FIGURE 3.1 An activity triangle describing the integration of BeeSign into inquiry activities, adapted from Engeström, 1987

a key mediator, and then 4) iteratively identify additional mediators and explore their relationships with prior mediators, adapting as needed. Thus, we begin by determining what students might seek to achieve in reaction to our provocations and new tools (their object of activity). At the same time, we identify the kinds of conceptual tools that fit with these new objectives and that, if appropriated, will change how the students reason about the topic. Having identified the tools and objectives, we turn to the social structures and classroom culture that motivate the students to seek these new objects and facilitate their appropriation.

In the case of BeeSign, we decided to narrow the field of possible mediators by using the conceptual framing of structure, behavior, and function (Hmelo–Silver et al., 2007) to organize our activities. We were originally interested in exploring the lifecycle of the bees, but because this did not advance our discussion of structure, behavior, and function, we relegated it to a secondary topic. However, complex systems require students to be able to continually explore different levels of a system as they relate to each other. This focus on levels appeared to be a natural fit with the stations approach that our collaborating teachers employed. We identified specific aspects of the system we wanted students to appropriate in each activity/station and then explored objects for their activity that we felt would help motivate their engagement with those concepts in productive ways. Finally, we iteratively explored how the mediators would help make this happen. In this process, orienting towards the rules, tools, and division of labor helped us reflect consistently upon the multiple dimensions of activity and incorporate both the material resources that we viewed as necessary and the kinds of social/ organizational rules that would help make this happen. For example, we decided to use students' drawings as a context for iteratively refining their understanding of the structures; we then decided to introduce a set of rules and division of labor through which students critiqued each other's drawings, helping them capture more details in an increasingly accurate manner.

The resulting set of interrelated activities was: 1) *drawing* activities where students could focus primarily upon the structures of the bees; 2) *participatory modeling* or role-play activities where students would act out the behaviors of the bees, thus focusing on those behaviors; 3) inquiry with the *BeeSign computer simulation* (Figure 3.2), which was intended to help students explore the function of the honeybee dance; and 4) a *nectar collection game*, which was intended to help students see the need for a bee dance by helping them recognize how hard it is to find nectar within their playground. Thinking about this as a collection of activities that were intended to complement each other helped guide ongoing design discussions as we explored conceptual challenges within the context of each activity. For example, the waggle dance can be viewed both in terms of what it looks like and how it affects the hive's nectar collection efforts. This organization of activities allowed us to cover the mechanics of the dance within the participatory modeling activities, and the function and resulting properties of the dance with the BeeSign software, and then to think about how each group of students needed to move back and forth between these activities to gain both perspectives.

Some Key Dilemmas

Although many design decisions were made, we briefly highlight a few and how our activity theory approach helped us resolve them.

Seeing Aggregate Behavior via BeeSign

One of the most challenging aspects of learning about complex systems is to recognize how a simple behavior (e.g., the waggle dance) can affect the entire hive. We decided early on that a computer visualization such as BeeSign would allow us to show the students the resulting patterns in behavior, and yet we also feared that students would not attend to the most important patterns without some form of scaffolding. How might we resolve this and help mediate the students' use of BeeSign to make sense of how bees collect nectar? The answer that emerged was once again to take advantage of tacit knowledge of the collaborating classroom culture (Spinuzzi, 2005) and reappropriate the successful rug time activities we had observed, rather than simply asking students to work individually at the computer. When using rug time, we knew we could rely upon the teacher as a mediator to help guide students through cycles of inquiry

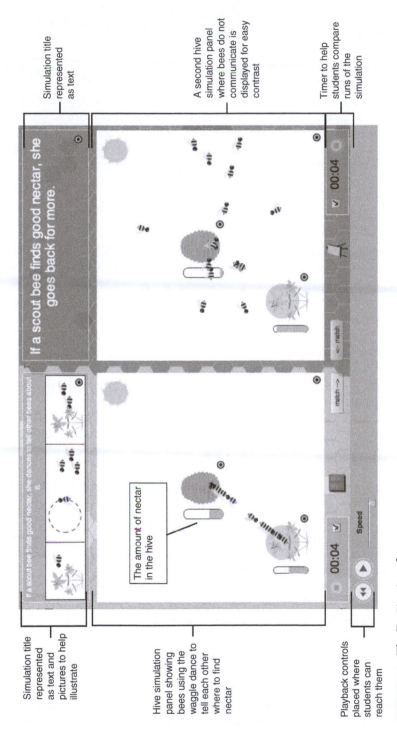

FIGURE 3.2 The BeeSign interface

Simulation title represented as text

A second hive simulation panel where bees do not communicate is displayed for easy contrast

Timer to help students compare runs of the simulation

Simulation title represented as text and pictures to help illustrate

Hive simulation panel showing bees using the waggle dance to tell each other where to find nectar

Playback controls placed where students can reach them

If a scout bee finds good nectar, she goes back for more.

If a scout bee finds good nectar, she dances to tell other bees about it.

The amount of nectar in the hive

Speed

00:04

00:04

match →

← match

that might help them see patterns in bee behavior. Therefore, we designed Bee-Sign to be a flexible tool that relies on the teacher's knowledge of inquiry and ability to work with students to move through multiple processes of observing and noticing. The activity triangle (see Figure 3.1) was then a powerful tool for helping us iteratively refine BeeSign to work with the teachers in this context. For example, if the teacher was going to use BeeSign on the whiteboard in front of the room, the interface needed to support work on a whiteboard and the possibility of students coming to the front of the room. As a result, we aimed for a simplified interface that could be seen at a short distance, but easily controlled by a child who could only reach halfway up the whiteboard.

Participatory Models Were Too Free

The participatory models where students role-played as bees were intended to help them explore bee behaviors in small group settings. We chose this kind of embodied activity because it allowed students to quickly and easily construct a series of models while thinking about what a bee would do by using their bodies. Early in our implementation, this worked quite well at helping students express their own ideas for us to discuss. However, we soon saw that although the students were motivated to be accurate, they did not actually constrain their behaviors to what real bees would do as they became lost in the moment and were acting out next steps within the current performance. For example, students did not like to be the bee that could not find nectar, so they would often "cheat," using their privileged knowledge of their peers' activity to claim they had found nectar, thus changing the model on the fly. During a weekly debriefing session with the teachers, we discussed this challenge and brainstormed alternative approaches that would remain true to our learning objectives. Together, we decided that we needed to find a way to *remediate* the students' performance in a way that would help the students use the content to constrain their activities. This resulted in two changes to our activity design.

First, we noted that because all of the students were part of the model, they had difficulty critiquing it. Therefore, we opted to change the division of labor, having students take turns as the model or as the audience. This idea was based in large part on the teachers' prior success in using an explicitly labeled audience during activities where students workshopped each other's writing. The audience members were asked to watch the model and offer critical scientific feedback. Second, we proposed providing a short script for the activity, intended to give the students more structure, but also allowing them flexibility in how to interpret the script. The teachers suggested that although the script could be initially helpful, the students should be encouraged to adapt the script and write their own, a revision that was incorporated in our final activity design. The combination of a script and an audience helped students engage in some of the previously less desirable roles such as finding a flower without good nectar, but also provided them with a reason (scientific accuracy) to include that and then discuss what the bee would do next (search for other flowers or return to the hive). Activity theory again helped us work with the teachers and explore how a change in the environment and rules necessitated a concomitant shift in the division of labor to support the outcomes we had in mind.

Design Story #2 Learning Physics through Play: Bridging Existing Activity Systems to Create Something New

Impetus

Unlike the BeeSign project, the LPP project was initially inspired by innovations in technology. The Center for Research in Engineering, Media, and Performance (REMAP) at UCLA approached us about the potential for collaborating on projects that would leverage new motion-tracking technologies that they were developing. Even though LPP was implemented after BeeSign, the many rounds of discussion, brainstorming, and grant writing began several years before Bee-Sign began. In fact, the role of bees in pollination was proposed as one of the early uses of the motion-tracking technology and ultimately informed aspects of the BeeSign curriculum.

A First Dilemma: Technology in Search of a Use

Although it is only obvious in hindsight, our first true dilemma in designing LPP lay in the fact that we began with a focus on technology rather than on learning and activity. It was particularly easy to conflate these ideas given that a few moments of interaction within the prototype tracking system demonstrated quite viscerally how the system could support the kind of enthusiastic, embodied, active, and playful interactions that we had long observed as central to the learning process within early elementary classrooms. It was easy for us to take for granted that the embodied activity supported by the motion tracking would be central to an effective learning design without initially challenging ourselves to propose a specific mechanism for how this would work.

As a result, we initially thought about the motion-tracking technology as a way to allow people to use their bodies and motions as a tangible interface to computer simulations and information. This led to a series of designs that were abandoned, either because we felt they didn't support learning in an innovative and interesting way or because they were declined for funding. Fortunately, we persevered, iteratively refining our designs in response to feedback from reviewers and in response to our continued exploration of both the classrooms in which we would ultimately collaborate and the technology we would use.

Early proposals included a design where students could explore the cholera epidemic of 1866 by wandering the streets of a virtual map of London and a simulation where students could shrink down to explore the impact of radiation upon human cells as a way to explore the problem of long-term exposure to radiation that currently prevents manned missions to Mars. However, these were quite technocentric and driven more by our ideas about how the technology might serve as a unique interface into a complex visualization than by an explicit reconsideration of how embodiment of this form may support learning in new and powerful ways. As we continued to brainstorm, we noticed that we had always intuitively designed for students to take on a role and participate within a simulation. We also began to notice and discuss the similarities between our proposed designs and sociodramatic play. At the same time we were using activity theory to conceptualize BeeSign as the integration of new mediators into existing activity systems. These ideas were quite salient in our reflection and discussion as we began to design the system that ultimately became the proposal for LPP.

Initially we turned to Newtonian motion because we thought that the congruence between objects in motion and bodies in motion would make for a powerful learning experience. Like our previous proposals, we began this one in a technocentric manner. However, the use of activity theory to shape the BeeSign project, now underway without motion-tracking technology, changed our process. We began looking for preexisting activity systems that we could build on in our process of anthropological activism and key mediators that we could use to promote this system-level development. Instead of starting with the classroom as the system we wanted to transform, we began with considering how the leading activity of childhood—play—could be developed and enriched through new forms of technology.

From a sociocultural perspective, the power of play stems from the fact that in play, children engage with both an *imaginary situation* and a set of *rules* (Vygotsky, 1978). The imaginary situation provides a unique context in which children are able to explore rules that might otherwise be obtuse or invisible to them. With motion-tracking technology, we could support new and distinct forms of play as a way of supporting science learning.

Conceptual Goals and Design

Many studies of play focus on "rules" about how to act and behave in everyday life, such as two girls playing at being sisters to better understand their own relationship (Vygotsky, 1978). Our goal was to instead have students focus on the "rules" of science and then develop new technologies to help them do just that. For our initial implementation, we selected the concepts of force and motion because they are well covered in the science literature, but are typically treated as the domain of much older students (e.g., middle and high school). Fortunately, young children have many experiences in the physical world that reflect an intuitive understanding of force and motion. All students in our study, for example, had experience kicking soccer balls or bouncing basketballs. The goal of the LPP project was to use motion-tracking technology as the basis of a mixed-reality environment that would allow students to explore these physics concepts by embodying them and then reflecting upon their own embodied play.

For example, one student would pretend to be a ball. Another student pretended to be a "force" such as a kick and would act this out with exaggerated gestures (but without kicking his or her friend!). The student-as-ball would then dramatize how he or she thought the ball would react, using his or her own experience of moving through space to show how a ball might roll in the direction of the kick. All of this activity could take place at the rug area and be tracked by our new LPP system, which projects a mixed-reality display of a simulated ball being kicked. What this means is that the students see a video of themselves play-acting as a ball and a "force" and at the same time can see a symbol of a ball and forces (arrows) overlaid on the screen; they can begin to think about their motion in symbolic and systematic ways, thus exploring the rules of the motion of an object subjected to a force.

When LPP was funded, we initially attempted to draw activity triangles much as we had with the BeeSign project. However, when we attempted draw classroom-level activity systems for a 15-week unit, we soon realized that the scope of the project resulted in a much greater number of activities than we had faced in BeeSign. There were too many ancillary activities—such as having students play skee ball to explore different levels of friction—for us to feel we could easily capture the detail we needed to support both our design and the presentation of curriculum materials to the teachers. Rather than drawing four triangles to represent four classes of activity, we found ourselves with dozens of triangles and intense (though friendly!) debates about how to be sure we documented the many nuanced activities that we wanted to support. We were once again stuck in the quagmire of wanting to attend to all of the features of the activity and not knowing how to make the problem more tractable.

Faced with an ever-expanding sequence of triangles, we decided that we needed to use activity theory at a different level than we had before. Instead of a series of activity systems that described the development of a classroom over 15 weeks, we returned to thinking about how we were transforming the activity of play into the activity of scientific modeling. This led us to reorganize our design around two principles: 1) providing opportunities for play as a form of scientific modeling, and 2) providing opportunities to progressively define and refine the symbols (i.e., key mediators) used in this system (Enyedy et al., 2012). These two principles can also be conceived of as two interrelated activity systems of the classroom (see Figure 3.3). The activity of modeling in small groups produces multiple models of the rules of Newtonian motion. This 'product' becomes the object of activity for students to progressively come to a consensus as a collective on the model that they currently think best represents their understanding. We asked them to inscribe key aspects of the model (force, friction, etc.)

Activity system 1: play-as-modeling within LPP

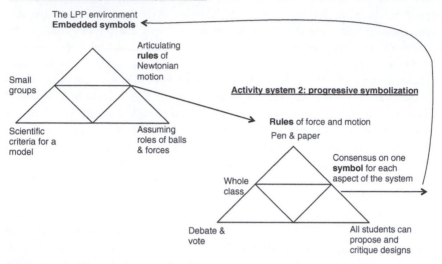

FIGURE 3.3 The two interacting activity systems in the LPP environment. The play in the LPP environment produces new rules that mediate discussions about progressive symbolization, which in turn produce new symbols for the LPP system.

into symbol systems that they and the computer could use in subsequent activity. Thus, the product of this second activity system refined the tools that the students used to engage in all future modeling.

A Second Example Dilemma: Only the Ball Articulated Decisions and Had Fun

We began our classroom implementation with this proposed cycle of modeling through play and progressive symbolization. As with the BeeSign implementation, however, we continued to meet regularly with the teachers to refine our designs. Once the students had become familiar with the technology, a new dilemma presented itself: the presence of only one ball in the space at a time. We had originally assumed that although being the ball might be the more desirable role, students would also enjoy the opportunity to be a "force" and employ overly exaggerated motions to convey the scale of the force. However, we soon realized that students had more fun when they were the ball and less so when playing force. More importantly, as our orientation towards the rules in play helped us to note, the student who played at being the ball was primarily the one who made decisions about the rules of the system and articulated them! Few of the other students voiced their understanding or debated them unless prompted by the teacher. We began to brainstorm solutions that would encourage more students to discuss and negotiate the rules of play. There were two kinds of rules:

those that structured students' activity (e.g., who got to move when) and those that were grounded in physics, which we wanted them to explore. By changing the former kind of rule, we could continue to influence the latter. We therefore devised a game where teams of students had to work together to determine how and where to place various sized forces to move a ball across the space and score a goal. The students continued to enact this and viewed the results within the LPP simulation, but having to negotiate the next step pushed the students to articulate their rules and make them visible throughout the activity.

Discussion

Both projects successfully allowed us to simultaneously support early elementary students in learning complex science concepts and to advance our theories about how to support these efforts. Taken together, they also helped us recognize the value and the challenge of using activity theory in design. We continue to view activity theory as powerful for supporting educational design because of the way it helps articulate the relationship between rich mediated contexts and student learning. However, we also recognize the challenges this introduces, as one cannot always take into account every single mediator, nor every single influence.

We have, therefore, used two very different approaches to resolve this problem, each grounded in the nature of the content being explored. In the BeeSign project, we wanted to help students look at a system from multiple perspectives. Activity theory provided a powerful tool for organizing activities around each of those perspectives and provided ways for us to articulate how the activities could be shaped to support appropriation of the target perspective. In contrast, our focus on a single set of continually refined rules in the LPP project was not as easily mapped by activity triangles. Nonetheless, our vision of play from an activity theory perspective, as necessarily including both rules and a division of labor, turned out to be a powerful organizing principle. We were able to move beyond the need to explicitly articulate each element of each activity by focusing on how they related to play.

References

Bødker, S. (2009). Past experiences and recent challenges in participatory design research. In A. Sannino, H. Daniels, & K.D. Gutierrez (Eds.), *Learning and expanding with activity theory* (pp. 274–285). New York, NY: Cambridge University Press.

Brown, A.L. (1992). Design experiments: Theoretical and methodological challenges in creating complex interventions in classroom settings. *Journal of the Learning Sciences, 2*(2), 141–178.

Carroll, J.M., & Rosson, M.B. (2007). Participatory design in community informatics. *Design Studies, 28*(3), 243–261. doi:10.1016/j.destud.2007.02.007.

Danish, J.A. (2014). Applying an activity theory lens to designing instruction for learning about the structure, behavior, and function of a honeybee system. *Journal of the Learning Sciences, 23*(2), 1–49. doi:10.1080/10508406.2013.856793.

Danish, J.A., & Enyedy, N. (2007). Negotiated representational mediators: How young children decide what to include in their science representations. *Science Education, 91*(1), 1–35.

Danish, J.A., Peppler, K., Phelps, D., & Washington, D. (2011). Life in the hive: Supporting inquiry into complexity within the Zone of Proximal Development. *Journal of Science Education and Technology, 20*(5), 454–467. doi:10.1007/s10956-011-9313-4.

Engeström, Y. (1987). *Learning by expanding: An activity-theoretical approach to developmental research.* Helsinki: Orienta-Konsultit Oy.

Enyedy, N., Danish, J.A., Delacruz, G., & Kumar, M. (2012). Learning physics through play in an augmented reality environment. *International Journal of Computer-Supported Collaborative Learning, 7*(3), 347–378.

Enyedy, N., Danish, J.A., & DeLiema, D. (2015). Constructing liminal blends in a collaborative augmented-reality learning environment. *International Journal of Computer-Supported Collaborative Learning, 10*(1), 7–34.

Hmelo-Silver, C.E., Marathe, S., & Liu, L. (2007). Fish swim, rocks sit, and lungs breathe: Expert-novice understanding of complex systems. *Journal of the Learning Sciences, 16*(3), 307–331. doi:10.1080/10508400701413401.

John-Steiner, V., & Mahn, H. (1996). Sociocultural approaches to learning and development: A Vygotskian framework. *Educational Psychologist, 31*(3–4), 191–206.

Kaptelinin, V., & Nardi, B.A. (2006). *Acting with technology: Activity theory and interaction design.* Cambridge, MA: MIT Press.

Mwanza-Simwami, D. (2013). Activity theory and educational technology design. In R. Luckin, S. Puntambekar, P. Goodyear, B.L. Grabowski, J. Underwood, & N. Winters (Eds.), *Handbook of design in educational technology* (pp. 176–188). London: Routledge.

Nardi, B.A. (1996). *Context and consciousness: Activity theory and human-computer interaction.* Cambridge, MA: The MIT Press.

National Research Council. (2012). *A framework for K-12 science education: Practices, crosscutting concepts, and core ideas.* Committee on Conceptual Framework for the New K-12 Science Education Standards, Board on Science Education, & Division of Behavioral and Social Sciences and Education. The National Academies Press, Washington, DC.

Papert, S. (1993). *The children's machine: Rethinking school in the age of the computer.* New York, NY: BasicBooks.

Spinuzzi, C. (2005). The methodology of participatory design. *Technical Communication, 52*(2), 163–174.

Vygotsky, L.S. (1978). *Mind in society: The development of higher psychological processes.* Cambridge, MA: Harvard University Press.

Witte, S.P., & Haas, C. (2005). Research in activity: An analysis of speed bumps as mediational means. *Written Communication, 22*(2), 127–165. doi:10.1177/0741088305274781.

4

THE CHALLENGE AND PROMISE OF COMMUNITY CO-DESIGN

Leah Teeters, A. Susan Jurow, and Molly Shea

Introduction

Some of the most critical commentary on design-based research is directed at its unidirectional, hierarchical approach to knowledge production and dissemination (Engeström, 2011). There is great interest in developing alternative strategies for creating more collaborative and participatory design methodologies that could open up empowering ways of knowing and acting, especially for communities that have been historically marginalized (Cammarota & Fine, 2008; Gutiérrez & Vossoughi, 2010). We need to design new ways for people to participate and become in the world. This is a challenge that we have embraced in our ongoing work with under-resourced communities organizing for better social futures. To develop more transparent approaches to design research, we present the typically "untold" strategies and challenges of our research alongside some of the successes. We focus on telling the story of how we have grappled with the task of developing methods for doing *equity-oriented* research with culturally and linguistically diverse communities. By equity-oriented, we mean research and design efforts that facilitate members of marginalized communities in gaining greater access to and control over resources to shape their own lives. In this chapter, we focus on our partnership with *promotoras*, community leaders who are striving to increase food access and social justice in their western U.S. neighborhood. We share how we learned to organize design-based research, developing interventions such as professional workshops and technology tools, so that it can be equitable both in its process and its outcomes.

Promotoras de salud is a community health worker model initially developed to connect underserved communities with healthcare and educational resources. Research on promotoras de salud indicates that although promotoras do not have advanced degrees, they can promote healthcare as successfully as professional health workers (Ayala, Vaz, Earp, Elder, & Cherrington, 2010). Without professional degrees, promotoras, who are mostly women, are a less expensive labor force.

Through our related research on the food movement, we became familiar with a variation on the promotoras de salud model. Impact (all proper names are pseudonyms), a nonprofit focused on increasing food access in a local community, South Elm, with limited access to healthy and affordable food, uses promotoras to connect with the neighborhood's largely Mexican immigrant residents. The promotoras work with community members to grow their own backyard vegetable gardens. Impact's extension of the traditional promotoras de salud model is part of a larger community-based effort to increase food access, empower residents, and develop a more robust neighborhood economy. Impact's backyard gardens produced more than 30,000 pounds of fruits and vegetables in 2014. The neighborhood now has over 300 gardens and a waitlist of over 100 residents who want an Impact garden, which includes an irrigation system, seeds, seedlings, and the support of a promotora throughout the growing and harvesting season. Impact has secured funding for the first community-run food cooperative in the city.

Impact's promotora model is compelling to us because it is a deeply cultural-historical model of community learning that has been extended, making connections to healthcare and education, to improve people's lives in the neighborhood. This type of community-led change has not typically been the focus of learning sciences research. Yet, it is this type of social change, built on the valued practices of community members, that has led to meaningful and lasting reform (Jason, 2013). Our interest is in understanding how the community organizes this change such that it can have a positive effect beyond the borders of the neighborhood and in generating participation structures and designed tools that support this process. Our design collaborations have been grounded in our interest in understanding community-based social change. The specific interventions we developed were driven by the needs and the desires of our community partners.

Focal Design Process Elements

The methods that undergird our research draw on insights from social design (Gutiérrez, 2008) and community-based design research (Bang, Medin, Washinawatok, & Chapman, 2010). These approaches seek to study learning *with* community members to focus on problems that are significant for the conduct of their everyday lives. These partnerships hold great potential for creating designs that are valued by communities; however, they are also rife with tensions that lie at the intersection of power and values in the organization of new learning trajectories. Community-based research brings together people from different social positions—typically those from the university and members of the community—generating working relationships that are asymmetrical in terms of access to financial, intellectual, and social resources. As members of the university enter into marginalized communities, there is a risk that asymmetrical power dynamics could generate relationships that invoke neocolonial models where outsiders engage in interactions with the 'other' with the intent of 'fixing' or 'saving' the community (Baker-Boosamra, Guevara, & Balfour, 2006). When participants speak a language other than that of the dominant culture, as is the case in our research, the potential for marginalization is even greater. An aim of our work is to avoid the reproduction of oppressive power relations while simultaneously trying to create opportunities with community partners to gain skills that could be valued across multiple contexts.

In developing a collaborative design project with our community partners, we organized our work around key focal design elements, including (1) negotiating roles to facilitate a participatory approach to design; (2) working across differences of language to develop equitable interactions; (3) using ethnographic methods to identify significant problems of practice; and (4) designing an equity-oriented intervention. In this chapter, we share the story of this design process, highlighting challenges we faced and how we managed, and are still managing, them.

Design Story: Organizing Equity-Oriented Design Research

As collaborative design researchers, we did not stand outside of the community and identify problems of practice for Impact, the promotoras, or the South Elm community. When we began our partnership with Impact, our initial focus was on learning about the promotoras and their role and work in the community. We developed a foundational understanding through a variety of means. We reviewed historical and contemporary artifacts (e.g., research articles on the public health significance of the promotora model and city newspaper reports on Impact's promotora model), conducted interviews with the promotoras and the Impact directors about their life experiences and motivations for their work, and conducted participant observation of the promotoras' work in the community. Our observations involved shadowing promotoras as they visited residents' homes to check on garden progress; performed their seasonal garden duties; and talked with residents about their concerns with the gardens, their family lives, and their experiences in the neighborhood. Through these observations, we came to know some of the Impact garden participants, and they were pleased to welcome us into their homes and share their stories with us.

Our initial analysis of ethnographic data highlighted the variance and ambiguity in how the promotoras defined their work. We realized that although the promotora model was successful in terms of establishing thriving backyard gardens, determining what exactly made it so was a genuine question for the promotoras and the nonprofit. For the promotoras, articulating their work was important so the expansiveness of their advocacy practices—which ranged beyond the gardens—could be acknowledged. For the Impact directors, articulating the promotora model was important so the model could be shared with other communities and used to appeal to funders. The questions that guided our work together were focused on the promotora model, why it works, and how it could be enhanced.

The story of our design process unfolded over 3 years. It began with getting to know each other and negotiating our roles as research partners. A key part of this process involved learning to work across differences of language background and interest in and knowledge of academic theory and method. Once we established routines for interacting together productively, we were able to identify a focal problem of practice on which we could center our design efforts and co-create a—potentially powerful—intervention. We discuss the challenges and successes we faced in this emergent design process.

Negotiating Our Roles

When we first began our design work with the promotoras and Impact, our research team wanted to be seen as equals, as collaborators helping the nonprofit address problems that mattered to the community. This was an ambitious and somewhat naïve desire on our part, as our partners did not yet explicitly understand the nature of our research aims nor of our skill set. Based on our affiliation with the premier state research university as professors and researchers in education, the promotoras and the nonprofit co-founders saw us as teachers, curriculum designers, and learning experts. We saw ourselves as researchers who wanted to work alongside community members to organize for learning that could lead to social justice. Although these goals are not necessarily opposed to each other, in our interactions with our community partners, these different perspectives conflicted in terms of defining our roles in the design collaboration.

As an example of the challenge of negotiating our roles, we share a scene from one of our first meetings with our community partners to plan a workshop series aimed at articulating the promotora model. Members of the research team tried to be very intentional about naming and acknowledging the expertise of the promotoras. As we saw it, the promotoras had expertise in relation to the content of community advocacy and gardening, and the research team had expertise in designing learning environments. Although the research team saw a shared sense of expertise as an essential feature of the co-design sessions, we did not realize that the promotoras' expectations and assumptions about our role as authoritative experts would need to be addressed explicitly. The following exchange captures some of the ways in which we tried to challenge this positioning to create new forms of participation between researchers and community members.

Turn	Role-Speaker (language)	Text
1	Researcher-Jurow (in English)	Everyone said communication is the most important. We need to talk to each other and respect differences, respect cultural differences, but it seemed like there was not an explicit way of talking about what you do. Everyone knows it is important, but it is kinda fuzzy.
2	Researcher-Teeters (translating from English to Spanish)	Todos decían la comunicación es la más importante. Tenemos que hablar el uno al otro y respetar las diferencias, respetar las diferencias culturales, pero parecía que no había una manera explícita de hablar de lo que haces. Todos sabe que es importante, pero es. . . . fuzzy.
3	Researcher-Teeters (in Spanish)	Nadie sabe realmente cómo hablar sobre cómo comunicar mejor. *No one really knows how to talk about how to best communicate.*
4	Promotora-Cuevas (in English)	Well, you (indicating the research team) have to teach us how. (Laughter)
5	Researcher-Jurow (in English)	Yeah, well, what I feel like, what we would need to do is to uncover what everyone is doing and what are the tensions.

The promotora's comment (turn 4) combined with the laughter suggests that there was a sense that the researchers' role was to provide expertise, "to teach" the promotoras how to do their job. The researcher's comment at turn 5 challenges this transmission approach by reframing the work that needed to be accomplished as a joint task ("what *we* would need to do," emphasis added) focused on the actual work of the promotoras. In making this statement, the researcher positioned the promotoras as experts on their job and the researchers as collaborators focused on helping the promotoras "uncover" what they are doing.

We developed a couple of strategies to challenge our positioning as experts working with novices: we explicitly stated our desire to collaborate and not to "teach" or be "experts" in relation to the promotoras; we arranged informal conversations over coffee instead of office meetings at a conference table; and we routinely visited backyard gardens, the primary site of the promotoras' work and where they are the experts. Being seen as collaborators was essential to our design work and was important for us to establish through our interactions with the promotoras.

Working Across Differences of Language

The opportunity to base our research in a neighborhood that had both a history of marginalization and a vibrant approach to organizing for a better future was very appealing to our research team. We were eager to embrace the challenges of working toward social justice; however, we were not fully prepared for what this would involve. In particular, we made two missteps at the start of our project: (1) not hiring a bilingual research team member who could help us communicate effectively with the primarily Spanish-speaking promotoras, and (2) not realizing how much our design discussions would rely on speaking English to talk about theory and technical elements of design.

The original research team members included two faculty members and one graduate student, none of whom was fluent in Spanish. We made the incorrect assumption that the promotoras would be able to speak English with us. This mistake was based on the fact that our negotiations to work with Impact had been conducted primarily with the English-speaking, White co-founders of the organization. As soon as we were face to face with the promotoras, we realized we would not be able to do our research without a Spanish-speaking member of the team. We decided to hire a community member to serve as a translator. Not only would this help us engage with the promotoras, we also believed that paying a community member to work with us would benefit our reputation in the neighborhood as people who could "give back" to the neighborhood and not only "take away." The community member we hired was recommended to us through the promotoras, and she helped us conduct initial interviews with the promotoras. What we soon realized, because we had some Spanish facility as a team, was that the translations were not exact and were problematic because the translator did not take up the details of the interviewees' words in her question formulations. Backing off our plan to hire a community member as a translator, we decided to invite a then–first year doctoral student (Teeters) who was bilingual, had taught in Mexico, and whose family was from the focal neighborhood to work on our project as a volunteer.

Even with a bilingual translator on the research team, language was still a significant challenge for our research. This was stressed to us one evening when the researchers met with the lead promotora to plan for a workshop focused on articulating the promotora model. Teeters, who served as our usual translator, was not available to attend the meeting. A bilingual doctoral student and native Spanish speaker served as a translator instead. The discussion lasted more than an hour and had gotten deep into the details of the sociocultural theory driving our design research with Impact. When the researchers paused for a moment to check in with the lead promotora and her perspectives on the discussion, she stated in a rare moment of frustration that it all sounded like "English, English, English." This comment was hard to hear and stuck with the research team. We realized that not only were we privileging the language with which we had most ease, but we were also privileging our interest in theory above the practical concerns of the promotora. This interaction led Jurow (the principal investigator) to offer Teeters an official position as a graduate student researcher on the team. This experience made us realize that not only did we need a translator who understood the theories and research methods that guided our work, we also needed someone who was deeply familiar with the promotoras' work and their cultural-historical experiences in the neighborhood.

Issues about language use are seldom only about language; they are also about the power relations embedded in historically established interactions between researchers and community members. When we used only English to talk about theory, we excluded the lead promotora from participating in a conversation that was fundamental to the design of the workshop. This was consequential for how promotoras could represent their work and its potential for improvement. This practice also reified the idea that English equals theory and Spanish equals practice, a social and linguistic hierarchy we wanted to avoid. We have learned over the years that our good intentions need to be turned into good everyday practices of interaction if we want to transform disempowering and historically entrenched patterns of research–community relations.

Identifying a Practical Problem on Which to Focus Our Design Efforts

We uncovered an unrecognized aspect of the promotora model through workshops investigating it, planning sessions in which we worked with promotoras to develop the workshop series, and our ethnographic analysis of Impact's effort. We learned that the promotoras' compassionate and sustained engagement with community members enabled them to develop a critical perspective of the needs of residents, the inequities facing their community, and a sense of responsibility as emerging civic leaders. This view was significant to the promotoras themselves; they routinely emphasized to us that the relationships they developed with community members were the foundation of Impact's success in South Elm (Jurow, Teeters, Shea, & Van Steenis, in press). They felt, however, that this was not fully acknowledged by the nonprofit leadership.

This expansive sense of being community advocates was relevant to the enactment of the promotora model because it shifted the promotoras' actions in the community. Their initial aim of establishing vegetable gardens had expanded to include a desire to challenge inequitable relations of power by reorganizing residents' access to social, educational, and economic resources (Jurow, Teeters, Shea, & Severance, 2014). The residents involved in the backyard garden program, many of whom are immigrants, turned to the promotoras as informal resources for information regarding medical care, legal troubles, and issues related to domestic violence.

Our growing understanding of the promotoras' unacknowledged and expansive enactment of community advocacy led to a shared desire to legitimize this powerful practice. The original aim to articulate the promotora model generated a practical problem of practice: how to develop a method for documenting the promotoras' extensive community advocacy work, as well as their work in creating a more just food system.

Designing an Equity-Oriented Intervention

Listening to the promotoras, we learned that, for them, designing for equity-oriented learning required developing tools that would (1) help them to collect systematic data on all of the important dimensions of their practice, (2) allow them to share and extend their knowledge, and (3) build on their valued cultural practices. The promotoras told us they wanted to develop business skills, such as grant and report writing, accounting, data management, and technical English language. The promotoras also expressed that they wanted more training in how to work in the gardens and in how to be better community advocates. These desires stemmed from their motivation to be viewed and treated as professionals.

Through sharing our emerging data analysis with the promotoras and the Impact leadership, as well as discussions with experts in the field of international development focused on women's empowerment, we came to see that technology could be a powerful tool in our design work with the promotoras. Faculty in the technology for development program on our campus suggested they could help us design a software application with the promotoras that could help them meet their diverse goals of collecting systematic data on their garden and relational work, gaining valued professional skills and representing their work to grant funders and policy makers. We presented Impact and the lead promotora with a proposal to design a tablet-based application that could allow the promotoras to enhance their practices while more fully representing and circulating their expertise across temporal, social, and spatial scales (Latour, 1983).

In keeping with our participatory and equity-oriented approach to design, we began the work of developing a software application using what Gutiérrez (2014) calls a *syncretic* approach to design. As she explains, a syncretic approach to design involves envisioning designs for learning that can both acknowledge the assets and practices of a community and extend them in more powerful directions. The outcome of these syncretic designs are tools, practices, and/or activity systems that strategically combine the historically valued practices of a nondominant community with those that are valued in established institutions to create potent practices that are empowering without being oppressive.

In order to design a tool that could codify the promotoras' knowledge and streamline data collection on their visible and nearly invisible forms of work, we partnered with our university's Information Communication Technologies for Development (ICTD) program. The ICTD students were learning to develop culturally responsive, sustainable technology tools in one of their lab classes. Our collaborative design sessions with ICTD students and promotoras were well intended, but in practice did not work out as we planned.

Although the ICTD students were from diverse ethnic and cultural backgrounds, they were all male and all monolingual English speakers. The technology team relied exclusively on English to discuss and debate the technicalities of the design of the software application. This form of discourse and interaction made it difficult for the promotoras, as well as the education researchers, to share their expertise and contribute to the design process. The design sessions, which were meant to be collaborative and dialogic, became expert-led and monologic.

In response to this failure of the face-to-face co-design efforts, Jurow and Teeters decided to remediate the design activities by meeting with the technology students and then brokering that knowledge to the promotoras. This allowed for one-on-one interactions that were not possible in a larger meeting dominated by English speakers. Moreover, this setting allowed Jurow and Teeters to build upon the trust they had established with the promotoras and to reorganize the interactions so that they could be both critical and oriented toward reflective action (see Freire, 1995).

These more personalized meetings were held with multiple promotoras at some times and with just the lead promotora at others. This allowed our team to learn about the promotoras' specific relationships with technology. For example, in one of the larger meetings, we discussed how to create the forms in an Excel spreadsheet before uploading the information to the application. It was not until we met in a smaller group that the lead promotora felt comfortable sharing that she had never used Excel. We were then able to provide her with training in it. Because the promotoras had facility with technology, but not always with the specific applications that we—as researchers—used, it was difficult to anticipate what they did and did not know. A more intimate setting allowed the promotoras to share their knowledge with us, such as correcting the forms to more closely align with the specifics of the growing season. Meeting in smaller groups was important to our participatory design work because it allowed us to share our mutual forms of expertise.

The collaborative, interdisciplinary design process that eventually emerged brought in the promotoras as designers, apprenticing them into practice (Lave, 1991). This process positioned the promotoras as novices with technology development and as experts in the community and in agriculture. This apprenticeship model also allowed the promotoras to be empowered with the skills to build technology, as opposed to simply being the recipients of designed tools. This deeply participatory approach mitigated the risk that our designs would further marginalize the promotoras.

The software application that we designed through this process is called the "Promotora App." The promotoras regularly use the application when they are in the community to collect quantitative data on garden productivity and qualitative data on their interactions with residents. The Impact team is now considering ways in which the data collected through the Promotora App can be integrated more fully into their assessment, training, and evaluation practices. The promotoras are also considering how they can participate in data analysis through the writing and creation of data reports.

Discussion

In our work with the promotoras and with Impact, our research team developed and tried out different strategies for creating transparent and equitable approaches to design work. We encountered challenges while negotiating equitable, participatory roles and outcomes, including working across differences of language and power and designing an equity-oriented intervention; these reinforced the importance of being explicit about research aims and approaches, and of being intentional about addressing issues of power and language. The emerging strategies have helped us address the challenges encountered as we developed our design process.

Our strategies were informed by Gutiérrez's (2008) "social design experiments" and Hall and Horn's (2012) writing on how representational infrastructure shapes what can be known, learned, and valued in a social setting. Perspectives on social change—drawn from sociology (e.g., Foucault, 1988), human geography (e.g., Soja, 2010), and economics (e.g., Sen, 1999)—also informed how we conducted our participatory design research. We also drew upon our experiences as teachers of native Spanish and English speakers. We did not set out with a predetermined approach to organizing our collaborative design work; yet, what we did was always deeply informed by theory and refined through ongoing and critical reflection on our process.

Through a disciplined yet improvisatory approach, we developed a productive relationship with the promotoras and designed a new tool (the Promotora App) that they use to collect systematic data in the field. The lessons learned through our design efforts speak to methods for organizing interactions between researchers and community partners that support productive co-design and the significance of ethnography for generating equity-oriented and sustainable designs.

Participation Frameworks for Supporting Co-Design

Our design research aimed to position the researchers and the participants as mutual collaborators. Although the research team and our community partners brought different expertise to the endeavor, as Erickson (2006) suggests, "studying side by side" in this way produces more authentic and holistic accounts of activity systems. By having the community members and researchers play a shared role in the design and the implementation of research, "ideas can be fed back, discussed, and negotiated as part of the ongoing practice of research" (Rogers, 1997, p. 69). The community members were positioned as experts in their work as gardeners and community advocates; their everyday interpretations and experiences were foundational to generating relevant problems of practice and sustainable solutions (Cahill, 2007). The researchers facilitated a reflective and action-oriented practice, propelling social change toward a vision of greater agency and equity for all participants. By positioning promotoras and researchers as mutual collaborators working toward the same goal, we worked to ensure that the emerging interventions, such as the Promotora App, were not imposed from the outside, but rather were embedded in existing practices.

Our co-design process involved identifying leaders within the organization who wanted to work in small groups with the researchers to design activities and tools to create expansive learning opportunities for all participants. Our goals were fluid. Our main goal was to open up opportunities for the promotoras to expand their practices, but our specific goals were not defined at the outset. For example, when developing workshops for the promotoras, we began by working with the lead promotora. She then identified two other leaders based on leadership traits such as charisma, work ethic, and vision. With these promotoras, we met to draft a plan for the workshop. The promotoras led by defining what they wanted the outcomes and process to be, and then we organized the design of the specific activities by drawing on our expertise designing learning environments. All participants took active roles in the process of determining the shape of the collaborative knowledge building (Rogoff, 1994).

We enacted a similar process of collaboration in designing the tablet-based application that the promotoras currently use to record data related to their work. We began with a small group of interested partners. The promotoras led by defining their vision for how the application would be used, and we, with support from our ICTD partners, helped lead the design of a solution. These two examples of design, the first of a learning environment (i.e., the workshop) and the second of a learning tool (i.e., the tablet-based application), illustrate how diverse forms of expertise can be used to complement each other in a co-design process.

Ethnographic Analysis of Promotoras' Practices

Our designs for expansive learning in this project were embedded in participants' existing practices, rather than imposed from the outside. We drew on the promotoras' everyday experiences as professionals in the community as well as our analysis of ethnographic materials to ascertain "what people have to know to do work, and how that knowledge can be deployed" (Button, 2000, p. 319). Our deeply collaborative approach allowed us to develop design interventions that could support the promotoras' work practices. For instance, the user interface of the application was designed to reflect digital media that the promotoras were already using, such as Facebook, and the drop-down items in the application were selected based upon observations and reports from the promotoras of the practices that they wanted to codify. This approach not only helped ensure the sustainability of the designed products and processes, but it was also integral to our commitment to equity. One of the main reasons designed interventions—especially technological tools—fail is because they do not take into account the contexts in which they will be used (Engeström, 2011). Designing tools that complement and expand existing tools have a greater likelihood to be used and sustained in practice. To the latter point, and more critically, embedding design solutions in everyday practices minimizes the chance that design solutions will be imposed in a top-down manner, invoking colonial models where outsiders present interventions with the intent of "fixing" or "saving" nondominant community members (Yapa, 1996). The long-term and multisited ethnographic work that we conducted in the local community, in the nonprofit office, and in the city and surrounding region informed our design decisions. The reflective way in which we engage in ethnography enabled us to understand participants' everyday practices and to understand which of those practices carry the most potential to open up new possibilities for future practices.

Toward Greater Transparency in Collaborative Design Research

As researchers in the learning sciences, our methodologies aim to respond to the need to address the situated and distributed nature of learning. We take up this challenge while foregrounding equity. We recognize that if we seek to generate equitable outcomes, the processes by which we enact change must be orchestrated such that equity is embedded in every stage. This deep focus on equity, as well as our intent of generating research designs that open up possibilities for new forms of future participation, necessitates that our research move beyond the confines of established institutions and into the dynamic contexts of community work and social movements for justice. In doing this work, we have been intentional and reflective about our design decisions so that we do not replicate historical patterns of marginalization.

How design decisions are made is an expression of historically developed values, dispositions, and perspectives on social change and learning. Different values, dispositions, and perspectives affect how designs are selected, implemented, and made socially significant (LeDantec & Do, 2009). Revealing how design decisions are made is important because it draws critical attention to issues of power and equity in the design of new collective possibilities. In this chapter, we have tried to reveal the typically untold processes of design. We drew critical attention to how we made design decisions in our routine practice: how we draw upon theory, how we refine and revisit our decisions, and how we have been responsive to community members' concerns. We coupled our commitment to rigorous design with a humble approach, recognizing the limitations of our tools and perspectives. This balance is always in progress. We need more conversations about how to do research *with*—as opposed to *for*—communities, designing powerful tools that can be taken up and sustained by communities themselves. Although opening up this conversation is imperative to generating more sustainable, more just research methodologies, it also involves risk. Revealing researchers'—at times—messy process of developing designs while simultaneously revealing the theoretical commitments that have informed design decisions and iterations is necessary to move towards generating a more honest, vulnerable, and equitable dialogue around research methodologies.

References

Ayala, G.X., Vaz, L., Earp, J.A., Elder, J.P., & Cherrington, A. (2010). Outcome effectiveness of the lay health advisor model among Latinos in the United States: An examination by role, *Health Education Research, 25*(5), 815–840.

Baker-Boosamra, M., Guevara, J.A., & Balfour, D.L. (2006). From service to solidarity: Evaluation and recommendations for international service learning. *Journal of Public Affairs Education, 12*(4), 479–500.

Bang, M., Medin, D., Washinawatok, K., & Chapman, S. (2010). Innovations in culturally based science education through partnerships and community. In M.S. Khine & M.I. Saleh (Eds.), *New science of learning: Cognition, computers, and collaboration in education* (pp. 569–592). New York, NY: Springer.

Button, G. (2000). The ethnographic tradition and design. *Design Studies, 21*(4), 319–332.

Cahill, C. (2007). Including excluded perspectives in participatory action research. *Design Studies, 28*(3), 325–340.

Cammarota, J., & Fine, M. (2008). *Revolutionizing education: Youth participatory action research in motion.* New York and London: Routledge.

Engeström, Y. (2011). From design experiments to formative interventions. *Theory & Psychology, 21*(5), 598–628.

Erickson, F. (2006). Studying side by side: Collaborative action ethnography in educational research. In G. Spindler & L. Hammond (Eds.), *Innovations in educational ethnography: Theory, methods and results* (pp. 235–257). Mahwah, NJ: Lawrence Erlbaum.

Foucault, M. (1988). *Madness and civilization: A history of insanity in the age of reason.* New York, NY: Random House.

Freire, P. (1995) *Pedagogy of hope. Reliving pedagogy of the oppressed.* New York, NY: Continuum.

Gutiérrez, K.D. (2008). Developing a sociocritical literacy in the third space. *Reading Research Quarterly, 43*(2), 148–164.

Gutiérrez, K.D. (2014). Integrative research review: Syncretic approaches to literacy learning. leveraging horizontal knowledge and expertise. In P. Dunston, L. Gambrell, K. Hadley, S. Fullerton, & P. Stecker (Eds.), *63rd Literacy Research Association Yearbook* (pp. 48–61). Alamonte Springs, FL: Literacy Research Association.

Gutiérrez, K., & Vossoughi, S. (2010). "Lifting off the ground to return anew": Documenting and designing for equity and transformation through social design experiments. *Journal of Teacher Education, 61*(1–2), 100–117.

Hall, R., & Horn, I.S. (2012). Talk and conceptual change at work: Adequate representation and epistemic stance in a comparative analysis of statistical consulting and teacher workgroups. *Mind, Culture, and Activity, 19*(3), 240–258.

Jason, L.A. (2013). *Principles of social change.* New York, NY: Oxford University.

Jurow, A.S., Teeters, L., Shea, M.V., & Severance, S. (2014). Transforming the scale of community advocacy in the movement for food justice. In B. Penuel, A.S. Jurow, & K. O'Connor (Eds.), *Learning and becoming in practice. Proceedings of the 11th international conference of the learning sciences*, Boulder, CO: International Society of the Learning Sciences.

Jurow, A.S., Teeters, L., Shea, M., & Van Steenis, E. (in press). Extending the consequentiality of "invisible work" in the food justice movement. In special issue edited by M. Bang & S. Vossoughi on participatory design research in *Cognition & Instruction*.

Latour, B. (1983). Give me a laboratory and I will raise the world. In K. Knorr-Cetina & M.J. Mulkay (Eds.), *Science observed: Perspectives on the social study of science* (pp. 141–170). London and Beverly Hills, CA: Sage.

Lave, J. (1991). Situating learning in communities of practice. In L. Resnick, J. Levine, & S. Teasley (Eds.), *Perspectives on socially shared cognition* (pp. 63–82). Washington, DC: American Psychology Association.

LeDantec, C.A., & Do, E.Y.L. (2009). The mechanisms of value transfer in design meetings. *Design Studies, 30*(2), 119–137.

Rogers, Y. (1997). Reconfiguring the social scientist: Shifting from telling designers what to do to getting more involved. In G. Bowker, S.L. Star, W. Turner, & L. Gasser (Eds.), *Social science, technical system, and cooperative work: Beyond the great divide* (pp. 57–77). New York, NY: Psychology Press.

Rogoff, B. (1994). Developing understanding of the idea of communities of learners. *Mind, Culture, and Activity, 1*(4), 209–229.

Sen, A. (1999). *Development as freedom* (1st ed.). New York, NY: Oxford University Press.

Soja, E.W. (2010). *Seeking spatial justice*. Minneapolis, MN: University of Minnesota Press.

Yapa, L. (1996). What causes poverty? A postmodern view. *Annals of the Association of American Geographers, 86*, 707–728.

5

LIVING IN THE FOURTH QUADRANT

Valuing the Process of Design

Brian K. Smith

Introduction

Herbert Simon described design as being "concerned with how things ought to be, with devising artifacts to attain goals" (Simon, 1996, p. 114). One of the great pleasures in doing design is the satisfaction of creating meaningful products and ideas. Another pleasure in doing design is just that—the *doing* of design. I suspect that most designers do design because they enjoy the challenges of understanding situations in the world and developing solutions to improve them. They may also cherish the "certainty of uncertainty," that the majority of designed objects will go through iterations and improve based on feedback that is typically unexpected or novel. The process of designing artifacts, presenting them to stakeholders and collaborators, and refining them based on feedback can be seen as a form of making sense of the world. In defining how things should be, designers have to make sense of the current world and employ "designerly ways of knowing" (Cross, 2001, 2007) to determine how to reach their intended goals.

There is a healthy respect for design in the learning sciences. For example, the design experiments championed by Brown (1992) and Collins (1992) led to further articulation of design-based research that many researchers use in their studies of learning interventions (Anderson & Shattuck, 2012; Barab & Squire, 2004; Cobb, Confrey, diSessa, Lehrer, & Schauble, 2003; Collins, Joseph, & Bielaczyc, 2004; Design-Based Research Collective, 2003; diSessa & Cobb, 2004). This work has led us to value not only the products of design, but also the iterations that led to the products. This is valuable because, as the chapters in the volume suggest, doing design is not easy.

Focusing on the products of design can oversimplify the effort it takes to *do* design. Making the difficulties (and pleasures) of doing design transparent may help future designers improve their practices. This does not simply mean how to choose better typefaces, implement better scaffolds in software, and other things related to the creation of an artifact. It also means talking more about the conversations that designers have with their constituents, how they learn to understand situations, how that knowledge leads to new insights, etc.

In the remainder of the chapter, I present some of the details behind a computer-based learning environment I developed as part of my doctoral dissertation. That work was done many years ago, but I documented each iteration in detail because, even then, I believed there was something important about capturing the rationale for changes in the software and curriculum. Before presenting that, I will say more about the need to *value the process of design* as much as we value the final products and evaluations that are published in journals and conference papers.

Design and Pasteur's Quadrant

Many researchers are familiar with a representation of scientific research published by Donald Stokes in the late 1990s. Stokes' notion was that the nature and purpose of scientific inquiry was more complex than a simple dichotomy between basic and applied research. He reformulated the one-dimensional basic/ applied view of research as a 2 × 2 matrix, with each cell representing two dimensions of inquiry: the quest for fundamental understanding and considerations of practical and societal use (Stokes, 1997).

Figure 5.1 illustrates the four quadrants and the researchers Stokes used to characterize them. The vertical axis represents the research contribution to advancing scientific knowledge, and the horizontal axis characterizes the practical utility of the research. The result is three different ways to classify the inspiration for research along with exemplary scientists:

1. Purely basic research as exemplified by the work of Niels Bohr, the atomic physicist
2. Purely applied research as exemplified by Thomas Edison, engineer and inventor
3. A combination of basic and applied research known as *Pasteur's quadrant.*

Louis Pasteur advanced scientific knowledge in chemistry and microbiology while also applying that knowledge to real-world applications such as vaccination and pasteurization. Hence, his quadrant is often seen as interesting because it combines theory and application. Unlike Bohr's pure atomic research and Edison's pragmatic engineering, the "use-inspired basic research" of Pasteur is highly desired in fields that seek to advance knowledge and societal benefits. Hence, researchers in education disciplines (e.g., Bransford, Brown, & Cocking, 1999; Fischer, Bouillon, Mandl, & Gomez, 2003; Hoadley & Van Haneghan,

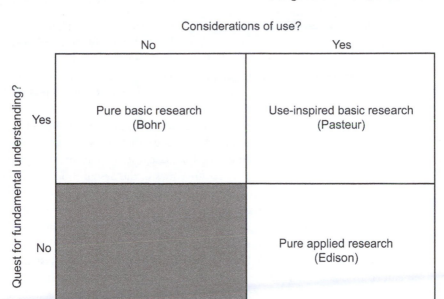

FIGURE 5.1 Stokes' representation of the goals of scientific research as advancing knowledge and/or solving dilemmas in the real world

2011; Mayer, 2008; Pintrich, 2000) have recognized that quadrant as an appealing place to situate their work, a hybrid place where theory and practice align.

However, I have always been interested in the unlabeled fourth quadrant. The lower left of the grid appears to be a zone where research is neither inspired by a desire to contribute to scientific knowledge nor to solve societal issues. People generally don't mention the mysterious, unnamed fourth quadrant when discussing Stokes' representations of research. When they do, it is typically pointed out as the quadrant to avoid because it appears to be void of theoretical or practical contributions.

Stokes explains that the quadrant is not empty. Rather, it is an area where particular phenomena may be explored for the sheer sake of exploration. He explains the value of research in the fourth quadrant as

> important precursors of research in Bohr's quadrant, as it was in the case of Charles Darwin's masterpiece *The Origin of Species*, as well as of research in Edison's quadrant . . . There are cases in which the prime goal of research is to enhance the skills of the researchers.
>
> *(Stokes, 1997, p. 75)*

In other words, there are times when research is conducted without a clear regard for or desire to produce publishable results. Investigations are often conducted in new or unexplored territory simply to develop new skills and experiences that may become useful in the future. Although the outcomes of these explorations are not as tangible as the light bulb or atomic structure, it would be unwise to ignore or downplay the importance of researchers working in the fourth quadrant to enhance their abilities in order to progress toward making new contributions.

It is unproductive to think of the fourth quadrant as an area populated by "failed" research. Instead, we should acknowledge that unexpected and/or unintended consequences are part of doing design, and it is often interesting to learn how designers deal with these. There are times in the design process when thinking and making must occur in order to generate more tangible artifacts and outcomes. In this sense, one can view the fourth quadrant as a necessary stage of research and design; it is the place where creativity and innovation begin.

I became more interested in the fourth quadrant during my tenure as dean of continuing education at Rhode Island School of Design (RISD). For instance, I remember a student showing me her attempts to design an innovative greeting card. She had constructed numerous iterations of her ideas in paper and had these on display. She eventually showed a finished concept, but she stressed the importance of working through tens of iterations before getting to the final version. I asked why she held on to dozens of prototypes since she had completed her work. She said that those iterative products were important because they inspired the final product.

She was not the only student I met at RISD who generated numerous sketches or physical forms before committing to the product ultimately displayed to the public. There was a deep respect for iteration, an appreciation that hard problems are unlikely to be solved on the first, second, or even third attempt. This is similar to Marples' observations of the role of iteration in engineering design; Marples observed that the design problem is knowable through solutions, and thus, considering only one solution "gives a very biased view," and that "at least two radically different solutions need to be attempted in order to get, through comparisons of sub-problems, a clear picture of the 'real nature' of the problem" (Marples, 1961, p. 64).

Valuing the process of design involves understanding that it is unlikely that any problem will be solved with the first solution one generates. It is much more likely that designers will use iteration to make educated guesses at a final solution, gradually learning more about the nature of the problem and potential solutions along the way (Cross, 2001, 2007). This is not necessarily evident if we only view design in terms of its end products—the artifacts that people ultimately come to use (or not use). However, if one views these artifacts as central to the research process, they become important representations of knowledge and understanding about certain phenomena. Carroll and Kellogg (1989) argued that designed artifacts are embodiments of psychological claims and, therefore, useful in the process of theory development and articulation. And Mäkelä (2007) suggested that an object can be viewed as the collection of knowledge and understanding that led to its creation by an artist, designer, and/or researcher, that making and what is made are tightly coupled to the creator's knowledge.

In this sense, we might think of design as a process of "knowing through making" (Mäkelä, 2007) where the iterative construction of artifacts incrementally increases a designer's knowledge. In fields like the learning sciences, designed artifacts are embodiments of theoretical perspectives on teaching and learning, individual and social cognition, etc. But the only way to truly unpack this knowledge from the artifact is to reflect on the processes that led to its creation. That process of making sense of the world through construction involves applying prior knowledge of design as well as learning new strategies, techniques, and patterns along the way.

Schön argued that designers engage in reflective conversation with design situations in which they frame and reframe problems. In these conversations,

> the practitioner's effort to solve the reframed problem yields new discoveries which call for reflection-in-action. The process spirals through stages of appreciation, action, and re-appreciation. The unique and uncertain situation comes to be understood through the attempt to change it.
>
> *(Schön, 1983, p. 131)*

These conversations live in the fourth quadrant, the place where designers actively make sense of problems and potential solutions. Although we ultimately want to move our work into a finished form and make contributions to basic, applied, and/or use-inspired research, we should acknowledge the learning that takes place in the fourth quadrant. In the next section, I discuss some of my adventures in that quadrant.

Design Story: Animal Landlord

As a graduate student, I was part of a project named *BGuILE* (Biology Guided Inquiry Learning Environments), a suite of software and curricula for teaching and learning biology (Reiser et al., 2001). Each of the curriculum units involved investigation activities that provided students with primary data that they worked to explain. The software was used to provide the investigation data and supporting scaffolds to assist analysis and explanation. The initial software implementations included *The Galapagos Finches*, a microworld where students learned about ecosystems and natural selection; *ExplanationConstructor*, a tool to scaffold student argumentation; and units on evolution (*TB Lab*) and conservation (*The Florida Panther*).

My contribution to BGuILE was the (oddly named) *Animal Landlord*. Initially developed for high school biology classrooms, students used the software to watch digital video clips of lions hunting their prey to learn about concepts in behavioral ecology such as resource competition, social cooperation, and foraging theory. The tools allowed them to annotate frames of video to create narrative explanations about how and why the observed animals might have evolved their behaviors. The flow of the tools had learners annotating video with key events, looking for variations in these events across videos, and finally creating explanatory models of the animal behaviors. The final version of the software and the investigation model that guided its design and empirical findings were reported in Smith and Reiser (2005).

The original software concept was very different from the program described in that article. And the video tools described evolved over four iterations, starting with small sessions in an on-campus laboratory and moving to larger implementations in Chicago-area schools. More than 300 students used versions of the software and its curriculum as we tried to understand the best ways to structure learning around the computer. I will describe details of some of these iterations to convey a sense of the conflicts that arose as we tried to understand how to design and integrate tasks and tools into the social context of the classroom to support causal reasoning about biological phenomena. More importantly, I want to show how our design process helped us identify and appreciate strengths and weaknesses of our artifacts and point the way to new solutions.

Animal Landlord as Simulation

After a review of the literature on biology education, we began developing the original version of Animal Landlord, a computer simulation of lion hunting that students could use to explore variables related to animal behavior. The program presented an aerial view of the Serengeti where students could observe simulated creatures going through hunting episodes. More specifically, they would observe multiple runs of a simulated environment and look for patterns that might explain the creature's behaviors. The simulated world facilitated experimentation, as students could manipulate behavioral variables attached to the creatures and see how outcomes differed as a result. Our simulated creatures could also explain their behaviors to help students understand what occurred during each run (Smith, 1996). We hoped that these explanations would focus student experimentation by pointing out interesting things to measure (e.g., How far from the prey is the lion when it begins to stalk?).

In the summer of 1995, we demonstrated a working prototype of the simulation to teachers. They worked with the virtual lions and zebras, but noted that it was difficult to know what students would *do* with the simulation. We worked closely with them to develop curricular activities around the simulated world, but they believed the exercise required additional constraints to make it useful for students. One concern was that students might not understand that models are abstractions of real events that can be used to test hypotheses (Grosslight, Unger, Jay, & Smith, 1991; Schauble, Glaser, Duschl, Schulze, & John, 1995;

Snir, Smith, & Grosslight, 1995). Another concern was that they might have difficulties understanding that models are created to test hypotheses about behavior, particularly since it is difficult to do such experimentation in the real world.

Some of the teachers mentioned that they showed nature documentaries in their classrooms, and most students enjoyed watching them. For the researchers, this resonated with the issue of helping students make connections between reality and a simulated model. Student familiarity with nature films could serve as useful introductions to the simulation tasks. I built a quick prototype where one could watch a video of lions hunting, grab frames that seemed important, and write explanations of those events (Figure 5.2). Work on guided questioning (Davis, 1996; King, 1994; Sandoval & Reiser, 1997) led me to add question-stems to the explanation window in order to focus students on relevant features of the films.

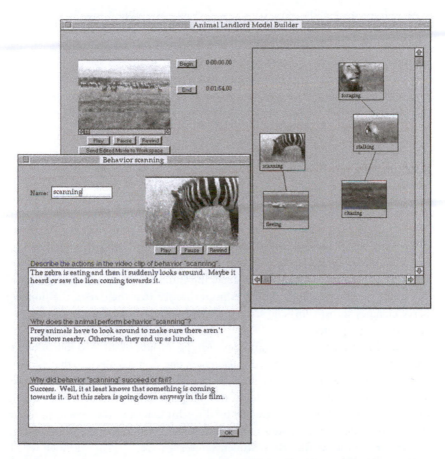

FIGURE 5.2 The first video prototype of Animal Landlord. A single film could be watched and decomposed into important events.

We demonstrated this prototype to teachers, and they felt that video might be a useful bridge to the simulation. I also discussed the prototype and teachers' suggestions with my peers and a visiting scientist in our lab, Susan Williams. We were working through the program one afternoon when Susan asked if it could be adjusted to let students watch multiple films. This simple suggestion changed the tool from a pre-simulation exercise to the core of the learning environment. Multiple films would allow students to compare hunting actions and look for variations in behavior that are a critical part of ecological and evolutionary theories. This meant that adjusting variables in the simulation to see variation was no longer necessary. The videos could serve as cases, and students could try to determine how similarities and differences in behavior led to different outcomes.

This represented a shift in our design process, what Wills and Kolodner (1994) referred to as *serendipitous recognition*, the process of viewing the design problem space from multiple perspectives in order to recognize possible solutions that may initially seem unrelated. This sort of design serendipity begins with problem evolution, the identification of features, attributes, and constraints of design problems. This evolving knowledge becomes assimilated into memory such that multiple alternatives can be compared, evaluated, and often selected as worthwhile pursuits. The role of video gradually increased as the initial problem space evolved and assimilation took place. Conversations with Susan and others led to the serendipitous recognition of a new design direction. And this led to new explorations of the modified design space.

Annotation

The transition to video began with selecting nine video clips to include in the software, each depicting different ways that lions obtain their prey. These 1- to 2-minute segments varied across factors such as size and composition of the lion/prey groups, prey species, time of day, hunting methods (stalking, ambushing), and hunt success or failure. This allowed students to make comparisons between films to identify strategic factors influencing hunt outcomes and their range of possible values. For example, students might notice that the size of the hunting party changes across films and that this could be related to the size of the prey animal being captured.

In the first trial of a new computer prototype, groups of three to four students worked with these clips, presented *without narration*, and an interface that allowed them to capture and annotate frames of the film to explain their significance. Their task was to develop a model of how lions (and their prey) behave during hunting episodes that would later be used to think about how evolution led to these behaviors. The first step towards this was interpreting and articulating plot structures for the film clips. Students observed visual events, decided which events contributed to hunting success or failure, and annotated each event with an explanation of its significance.

The results were not what I expected (Figure 5.3). Some groups watched the films, grabbed the final frame, and gave a single explanation about the success or failure of the hunt. Others broke the film down into several intermediate events, but their explanations were simply descriptions of what was happening in the

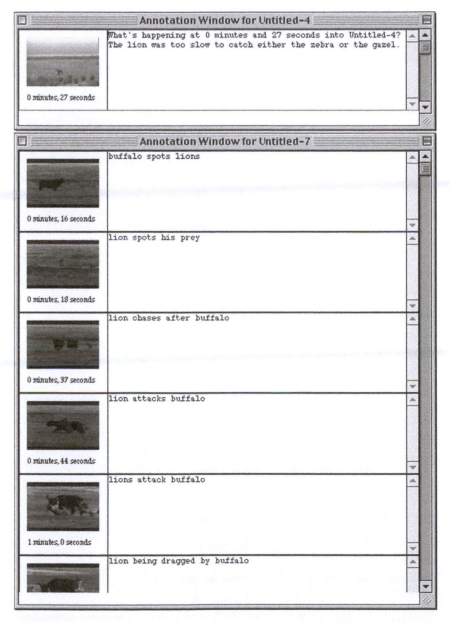

FIGURE 5.3 Annotations produced by students in the first video trials of Animal Landlord

frame (e.g., "Buffalo spots lions"). These were not wrong answers per se. In fact, they resembled the kinds of narrations one might hear in a documentary film. However, they were not the scientific explanations for which I had hoped.

Our teacher collaborators suggested that students were not accustomed to decomposing complex behaviors into constituent parts and would think of hunting as a simple outcome—the predator eats or goes hungry. Our initial implementation probed this hypothesis by giving students a QuickTime movie viewer coupled to a text document. Students could click a button to transfer the current video frame to the text document for annotation. We noticed some students would grab the final frame of the video and make comments such as, "The lion failed its hunt because it was slower than the warthog." In talking to the students who produced these minimal annotations, they seemed aware of other influences on the hunts, but they were accustomed to articulating final outcomes rather than causal relationships.

To address this final outcomes focus, we modified the movie browser to include a menu with possible actions, for example, "Predator stalks prey" (Figure 5.4). I thought that providing explicit suggestions about possible events would help students understand that many behaviors are responsible for the outcome of a hunt. We also constructed some introductory videos that we walked through

FIGURE 5.4 The action selection menu in Animal Landlord contained actions listed most likely to occur across a range of lion hunts and a way to add more events

with the entire class to practice making observations of behavior. Finally, questions were developed to guide discussions after students had made their first annotations of the films.

These changes were implemented in our next trial in high school classrooms and resulted in more detailed annotations. There were no longer single explanations at the end of a film; the action menu and introductory videos seemed to convey that a hunting episode consisted of multiple events. The explanations themselves were a bit more focused as a result, but they were still explanations of a single film rather than a more generalized account of predator–prey interactions. We had multiple films for students to annotate, but we lacked an explicit structure or process for them to compare and contrast what they saw in the clips. This became the focus of our next iteration.

Decision Trees

Comparison, both within and between species, is a useful technique for understanding animal behavior (Altmann, 1974; Martin & Bateson, 2004), and we wanted to help students observe multiple films and articulate similarities and differences that might be scientifically important. One instance of these productive discussions about variation occurred in a classroom where a group of students asked the teacher if cheetahs are better hunters than lions. The differences in speed, social organization, hunting success, and so on allowed the students to consider how natural selection could lead to behavioral differences between the two species. In reflecting on this discussion with a teacher, we realized that comparing the lion to other animals could be a useful way to facilitate additional reflection about the lions themselves.

We reasoned the first step would involve finding an appropriate animal for comparison. During the process of developing the curricula and software, I learned a lot about predation in mammals. My reviews of the ecological literature led me to chimpanzees and their occasional tendency to hunt red colobus monkeys. They do this in groups and successfully capture their prey 90% of the time (Stanford, Wallis, Mpongo, & Goodall, 1994). When I mentioned this to a teacher, she showed me a Sir David Attenborough documentary showing chimps hunting and killing a monkey in the wild. We immediately decided to show this footage during the first class session, and it became a core example used throughout the work to demonstrate how to make scientific comparisons.

In a way, the chimpanzee was another instance of serendipitous recognition. In similar, opportunistic fashion, the introduction of decision trees came from reading the ecology literature while thinking about ways to help students make comparisons. Predator–prey interactions can be represented as probabilistic models and depicted graphically as flowcharts or trees (Lima, 1987; Lima & Dill, 1990; Mech, 1970). Each node in the tree represents an action (e.g., "predator chases prey"), and the nodes feed forward to other possible actions (e.g., "predator kills prey," "prey escapes predator"). A more detailed model would place conditional probabilities on the arcs between nodes and, ultimately, compute a likelihood of success or failure based on paths through the tree. I was not interested in that level of detail, but the graphical representation appeared to be a useful way to generalize some of what students were seeing in the video clips.

To do this, we designed a jigsaw exercise (Aronson, 1978; Brown et al., 1993) to facilitate argument around the content of the annotations. As before, students were annotating films in groups, but we now assigned two videos to each group. After initially annotating those, the groups would divide and be recombined so that they had annotations for three films. That is, each new group had been assigned one film in common and two different ones. The hope was that there would be differences in the group's annotations for the shared movie. Students would have to determine where they disagreed and try to resolve those differences.

Once they discussed similarities and differences in the lion behaviors, we asked them to create decision trees. Each group received large sheets of poster paper to draw the tree by combining their annotations (Figure 5.5). These were placed around the classroom for others to see and teachers to comment on. This activity was the first time we saw students comparing events across films. Groups exchanged ideas and revised their explanations based on feedback from other

FIGURE 5.5 A decision tree created by a group in the second classroom trial of Animal Landlord

groups. A new sort of activity was emerging; namely, students engaged in a form of *remixing* as they annotated and developed explanations for the video fragments. During the construction of the decision trees, they became media critics, arguing about the validity of each other's annotations. The software played the role of a conversational prop in these encounters, a way for students to back their critiques with evidence. It was common to see students going back to the original video clips to argue about some aspect of behavior—"The lion trips *here*, and the wildebeest trips *there*, and *that's* how it makes the kill."

Discussion

Although I documented the design iterations behind Animal Landlord, this was the first time that I considered them in light of Stokes' characterizations of the aims of scientific research. In doing so, I realized the version of Animal Landlord described in Smith & Reiser (2005) might be thought of as my "fifteen minutes of fame in Pasteur's Quadrant." That paper described a knowledge contribution—an investigation model to support student observation and explanation of complex behaviors—and an applied contribution—the designed tools, curriculum, and classroom practices. In that sense, the paper positioned the design and studies as a form of *use-inspired basic research*.

But there were moments when aspects of the research could be located in other quadrants. For example, the use of artificial intelligence (AI) techniques to generate explanations of simulated behavior (Smith, 1996) could be placed in Edison's Quadrant. That stage of the research focused more on the applied aspects of the software, but it was grounded in existing AI theories. And I would argue that the majority of the design efforts were spent in the fourth quadrant, the area that Stokes noted as important for the development of new skills and insights. The iterative work that occurred in that quadrant was instrumental in understanding the design space enough to recognize opportunities that might otherwise be seen as failures.

Rather than formulating Stokes' quadrants as a static representation of a completed artifact's contributions, we can acknowledge that the design process likely moves through multiple quadrants as concerns for theory and application evolve over time. Thus, the plane containing the quadrants represents the aims of the artifact as a single point in time. One can imagine a rectangular volume consisting of planes divided into the four quadrants. The intermediate goals of research are captured on the planar quadrants, and the volume is a representation of the design process. Figure 5.6 illustrates how a design activity might move through different quadrants over time.

The path through the quadrants, the process of design, was influenced by the emergent behaviors of students and teachers as they worked through iterations of the materials. Along that path were instances of serendipitous recognition, moments when new opportunities appeared that changed the design trajectory.

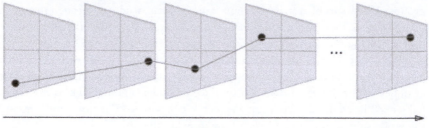

time *t*

FIGURE 5.6 Representing the intermediate goals in the design process as a series of planes over time. Each dot on a plane positions the designed artifact within one of Stokes' four quadrants.

For example, the shift from simulation to video environment may seem random unless you trace the path between iterations to understand the factors that led to the latter's emergence.

Indeed, video and the accompanying scaffolds would have never been developed without the conversations and observations that began with the simulation. It established theoretical and practical assumptions that were refined over multiple iterations. For example, teachers expressed concerns about the environment being too open-ended, too lengthy to fit into a week (or less) of class and lacking work products they would be able to assess. Learning these issues through the simulation allowed these to be reflected in future iterations. In this way, the design of the simulation was an important step in knowing through making.

Although much is learned from summative evaluations, it is equally useful to consider the emergent, often-serendipitous path that leads to design solutions. If we consider the process of design as a series of moves among the quadrants—including the fourth quadrant—it may be easier to see "failures" as learning opportunities and feel more comfortable with prototypes being steps towards bigger and better solutions. Additionally, if we think of design as a process of meaning making, it is important to understand the decisions that led to particular designs and the reasoning that suggested those decisions were appropriate (MacLean, Young, & Moran, 1989). The important thing is that we come to understand and value the design process enough to document how and why iterations are made.

References

Altmann, J. (1974). Observational study of behavior: Sampling methods. *Behaviour, 49*(3/4), 227–267.

Anderson, T., & Shattuck, J. (2012). Design-based research: A decade of progress in education research? *Educational Researcher, 41*(1), 16–25. doi:10.3102/0013189x11428813.

Aronson, E. (1978). *The jigsaw classroom.* Beverly Hills, CA: Sage Publications.

Barab, S., & Squire, K. (2004). Design-based research: Putting a stake in the ground. *Journal of the Learning Sciences, 13*(1), 1–14.

Bransford, J.D., Brown, A.L., & Cocking, R.R. (1999). *How people learn: Brain, mind, experience, and school.* Washington, DC: National Academy Press.

Brown, A.L. (1992). Design experiments: Theoretical and methodological challenges in creating complex interventions in classroom settings. *The Journal of the Learning Sciences, 2*(2), 141–178.

Brown, A.L., Ash, D., Rutherford, M., Nakagama, K., Gordon, A., & Campione, J.C. (1993). Distributed expertise in the classroom. In G. Solomon (Ed.), *Distributed cognitions: Psychological and educational considerations* (pp. 188–228). New York, NY: Cambridge University Press.

Carroll, J.M., & Kellogg, W. (1989). Artifact as theory-nexus: Hermeneutics meets theory-based design. *ACM SIGCHI Bulletin, 20*(SI), 7–14.

Cobb, P., Confrey, J., diSessa, A., Lehrer, R., & Schauble, L. (2003). Design experiments in educational research. *Educational Researcher, 32*(1), 9–13.

Collins, A. (1992). Toward a design science of education. In E. Scanlon & T. O'Shea (Eds.), *New directions in educational technology* (pp. 15–22). Berlin: Springer Verlag.

Collins, A., Joseph, D., & Bielaczyc, K. (2004). Design research: Theoretical and methodological issues. *Journal of the Learning Sciences, 13*(1), 15–42.

Cross, N. (2001). Designerly ways of knowing: Design discipline versus design science. *Design Issues, 17*(3), 49–55. doi:10.1162/074793601750357196.

Cross, N. (2007). *Designerly ways of knowing.* Basel, Switzerland: Birkhäuser Verlag AG.

Davis, E. (1996). *Metacognitive scaffolding to foster scientific explanations.* Paper presented at the Annual Meeting of the American Educational Research Association, New York, NY.

Design-Based Research Collective. (2003). Design-based research: An emerging paradigm for educational inquiry. *Educational Researcher, 32*(1), 5–8.

diSessa, A., & Cobb, P. (2004). Ontological innovation and the role of theory in design experiments. *Journal of the Learning Sciences, 13*(1), 77–103.

Fischer, F., Bouillon, L., Mandl, H., & Gomez, L. (2003). Scientific principles in pasteur's quadrant: Integrating goals of understanding and use in learning environment research. In B. Wasson, S. Ludvigsen, & U. Hoppe (Eds.), *Designing for change in networked learning environments: Proceedings of the international conference on computer support for collaborative learning 2003* (pp. 493–502). New York, NY: Springer Science+Business Media.

Grosslight, L., Unger, C., Jay, E., & Smith, C.L. (1991). Understanding models and their use in science: Conceptions of middle and high school students and experts. *Journal of Research in Science Teaching, 28*(9), 799–822.

Hoadley, C., & Van Haneghan, J. (2011). The learning sciences: Where they came from and what it means for instructional designers. In R.A. Reiser & J.V. Dempsey (Eds.), *Trends and issues in instructional design and technology* (pp. 53–63). New York, NY: Pearson.

King, A. (1994). Guiding knowledge construction in the classroom: Effects of teaching children how to question and how to explain. *American Education Research Journal, 31*(2), 338–368.

Lima, S.L. (1987). Vigilance while feeding and its relation to the risk of predation. *Journal of Theoretical Biology, 124*, 303–316.

Lima, S.L., & Dill, L.M. (1990). Behavioral decisions made under the risk of predation: A review and prospectus. *Canadian Journal of Zoology, 68*, 619–640.

MacLean, A., Young, R.M., & Moran, T.P. (1989). Design rationale: The argument behind the artifact. In K. Bice & C. Lewis (Eds.), *CHI'89 proceedings of the SIGCHI conference on human factors in computing systems* (pp. 247–252). New York, NY: ACM Press.

Mäkelä, M. (2007). Knowing through making: The role of the artefact in practice-led research. *Knowledge, Technology and Policy, 20*(3), 157–163.

Marples, D.L. (1961). The decisions of engineering design. *IRE Transactions on Engineering Management, EM-8*(2), 55–71.

Martin, P., & Bateson, P. (2004). *Measuring behaviour: An introductory guide.* Cambridge, UK: Cambridge University Press.

Mayer, R.E. (2008). Applying the science of learning: Evidence-based principles for the design of multimedia instruction. *American Psychologist, 63*(8), 760–769.

Mech, L.D. (1970). *The wolf: The ecology and behavior of an endangered species.* Garden City, NY: Natural History Press.

Pintrich, P.R. (2000). Educational psychology at the millenium: A look back and a look forward. *Educational Psychologist, 35*(4), 221–226.

Reiser, B.J., Tabak, I., Sandoval, W.A., Smith, B.K., Steinmuller, F., & Leone, A.J. (2001). Bguile: Strategic and conceptual scaffolds for scientific inquiry in biology classrooms. In S.M. Carver & D. Klahr (Eds.), *Cognition and instruction: 25 years of progress* (pp. 263–305). Mahwah, NJ: Lawrence Erlbaum Associates.

Sandoval, W.A., & Reiser, B.J. (1997). *Evolving explanations in high school biology.* Paper presented at the Annual Meeting of the American Educational Research Association, Chicago, IL.

Schauble, L., Glaser, R., Duschl, R.A., Schulze, S., & John, J. (1995). Students' understanding of the objectives and procedures of experimentation in the science classroom. *The Journal of the Learning Sciences, 4*(2), 131–166.

Schön, D.A. (1983). *The reflective practitioner: How professionals think in action.* New York, NY: Basic Books.

Simon, H.A. (1996). *The sciences of the artificial* (2nd ed.). Cambridge, MA: The MIT Press.

Smith, B.K. (1996). Why dissect a frog when you can simulate a lion? *Proceedings of the 13th national conference on artificial intelligence* (pp. 1372). Menlo Park, CA: AAAI Press.

Smith, B.K., & Reiser, B.J. (2005). Explaining behavior through observational investigation and theory articulation. *Journal of the Learning Sciences, 14*(3), 315–360.

Snir, J., Smith, C., & Grosslight, L. (1995). Conceptually enhanced simulations: A computer tool for science teaching. In D.N. Perkins, J.L. Schwartz, M.M. West, & M.S. Wiske (Eds.), *Software goes to school: Teaching for understanding with new technologies* (pp. 106–129). New York, NY: Oxford University Press.

Stanford, C.B., Wallis, J., Mpongo, E., & Goodall, J. (1994). Hunting decisions in wild chimpanzees. *Behaviour, 131*(1–2), 1–18.

Stokes, D. (1997). *Pasteur's quadrant: Basic science and technological innovation.* Washington, DC: Brookings Institution Press.

Wills, L.M., & Kolodner, J.L. (1994). Explaining serendipitous recognition in design. In A. Ram & K. Eiselt (Eds.), *Proceedings of the sixteenth annual conference of the cognitive science society* (pp. 940–945). Hillsdale, NJ: Lawrence Erlbaum Associates.

6

LOOKING UNDER THE HOOD

Productive Messiness in Design for Argumentation in Science, Literature, and History

Mon-Lin Ko, Susan R. Goldman, Joshua Radinsky, Katherine James, Allison Hall, Jacquelynn Popp, Michael Bolz, and MariAnne George

Introduction

Design-based research (DBR) as theorized within the learning sciences (Brown, 1992; The Design-Based Research Collective, 2003) aims to enhance our theoretical understanding of mechanisms and processes of learning, while grounding inquiry in improving learning in situ in real-world learning environments. Early DBR efforts reflected tension between the application of systematic, rational, "scientific" methods and an "argumentative participatory process in which designers are partners with the problem owners" (Cross, 2007, p. 2). Design fields use "designerly ways of thinking and communicating" (Archer, 1979, p. 17), a view recently embraced by DBR. But the origins and evolutions of these conjectures in the process of design decisions and implementation–revision cycles are often hidden in publications that conform to "scientific" explication of design rationales, learning outcomes, and theoretical insights (e.g., Barab et al., 2007). The conceptual and practical dilemmas wrestled with in a participatory design process are left "under the hood" and not discussed.

In this chapter we look under the hood to provide a glimpse into the productive messiness that occurred in the context of a large, multidiscipline, multistakeholder development and research project: READI (Reading, Evidence, and Argumentation in Disciplinary Instruction), a 5-year project funded in 2010 as one of six projects comprising the U.S. Department of Education Institute for Education Sciences' (IES) Reading for Understanding initiative. READI defined reading for understanding as evidence-based argumentation with multiple sources of information, situated within three disciplines—science, literary reading, and history.

Although we began with a consensus at a general level regarding design conjectures (e.g., instructional principles, materials, tools, task structures, discursive practices) and theoretical conjectures about how the designs would lead to the desired outcomes, our participatory design process brought to light multiple often fuzzy and conflicting conjectures about how specific tools, materials, etc., were going to mediate particular learning outcomes (cf. Figure 6.1, Sandoval, 2014). When it came to actual design decisions, we engaged in "messy" discussions that led to productive clarification and refinement of our thinking about not only how to support student learning, but also the very nature of what students needed to know and be able to do to engage in argumentation in the three disciplines. In this chapter, we illustrate the productive messiness of design decisions around tools to support students' grasp of the fundamental elements of argumentation—claims, evidence, and the reasoning connecting them. We elaborate first on the overall context of Project READI because it introduced several constraints on the design process.

Design Context: Project READI

Requirements of the IES call for proposals shaped the research and design space for READI. Citing a lack of educational research that effectively addressed reading comprehension beyond the basics of learning to decode, IES called for 5-year proposals to conduct (1) basic research contributing to theories of complex comprehension and informing the development of instructional interventions; (2) iterative cycles of design and revision to inform basic research; and (3) randomized controlled trials with the interventions. To maximize the likelihood of interventions affecting classroom practice, practitioners were to be among the project personnel from the inception of the project. READI targeted adolescents from ages 12 (6th grade in the United States) to 18 (12th grade).

Project teams were free to define reading for understanding as they wished. The READI definition highlighted two considerations often overlooked: the literacy demands of integrating across sources and the specific disciplinary norms and practices governing knowledge production and communication (e.g., Gee, 1992; Goldman & Bisanz, 2002; Lee & Spratley, 2010), such as criteria for sound arguments (e.g., Toulmin, Rieke, & Janik, 1984) and expected forms of information representations (e.g., texts and visuals).

We proposed to design Evidence-Based Argumentation (EBA) modules that would provide students with inquiry tasks that scaffolded opportunities to develop the knowledge, skills, and practices needed to engage with sources of information typical of each discipline. These included traditional verbal texts and diverse "text" forms such as photographs, diagrams, maps, and simulations (cf., Goldman, 2012; Lee & Spratley, 2010; New London Group, 1996).

READI personnel were organized into design teams for each discipline plus a basic studies group. Design team members represented multiple scholarly and professional perspectives: university-based researchers in the learning sciences, education, and/or psychology; curriculum and professional development designers; disciplinary experts; and classroom teachers (Voogt et al., 2015).

In this chapter, we illustrate the productive messiness of our participatory design process for one component of the larger effort: Evidence and Interpretation (E/I) charts, a tool we conjectured would support students in differentiating claims from evidence. The design of these charts in each discipline evolved through the productive messiness of our participatory design process and efforts to iteratively refine and clarify our conjectures about how the designs were expected to lead to intended outcomes. Our struggles over the "best" way to design these charts and activities around them led to insights into the dynamic nature of disciplinary inquiry and instruction that supports it.

Design Story

Initial EBA Design Efforts

The incompleteness of our general-level design and theoretical conjectures emerged soon after the grant was awarded and disciplinary teams attempted to develop concrete work plans and timelines for basic studies and designed modules. Across the teams, suggestions for tasks, texts, and support tools made by one team member were met with questions and counterproposals from other team members. For example, in the history team, some wanted to pose questions that asked students to make judgments about particular historical events (e.g., "Was the United States justified in intervening in Vietnam?"). Others proposed questions aimed at causal explanations for historical events (e.g., "What events and circumstances led the United States to send troops to Vietnam?"). These debates reflected differences in experience (e.g., classroom versus laboratory), disciplinary orientation (e.g., English language arts versus science education versus psychology), and methodological commitments (e.g., experimental versus ethnographic paradigms). At the first meeting of the whole team 3 months after the grant began, each disciplinary team attempted to provide the others with a sense of argumentation in that discipline. From this attempt to establish common ground emerged the need to be explicit about the competencies—the knowledge, skills, and practices—involved in evidence-based argumentation in each discipline. The hope was that this would allow a clearer articulation of the similarities and differences in disciplinary argumentation and set the stage for specification of the intended outcomes of the interventions.

Each disciplinary team worked on these separately, mining research literature and existing designs. We identified an overarching similarity: five categories of *core constructs* appropriate for capturing the competencies for each discipline: (1) epistemology (what counts as knowledge/how do we know what we know); (2) inquiry practices/strategies of reasoning; (3) overarching concepts, themes, and frameworks; (4) forms of information representation/types of texts; and (5) discourse and language structures that are invoked in comprehending and constructing arguments from evidence found in texts. The specifics within each category were particular to the discipline (Goldman et al., submitted). However, we found that there was little research about developmental similarities and differences in these competencies across the adolescent grade band.

The whole READI team also generated an initial list of "design principles" (more accurately, design features) that we agreed to incorporate into EBA designs in all three disciplines. These were derived from work of our own and others (e.g., Bransford, Brown, & Cocking, 2000; Britt & Aglinskas, 2002; Donovan & Bransford, 2005; Goldman, Braasch, Wiley, Graesser, & Brodowinska, 2012; Lee, 2007; Radinsky, Loh, & Lukasik, 2008; Schoenbach, Greenleaf, & Murphy, 2012; Shanahan & Shanahan, 2008; Wiley & Voss, 1999). In the following list, the first eight refer to features of topics, texts, and tasks and the remaining six to tools or scaffolds that guide the design and realization of classroom instruction:

1. Draw on core constructs, addressing at least one aspect of each of the five types of elements.
2. Text set informs the causal model for the phenomenon or event in science and history but poses interpretive problems in literature.
3. Integration across multiple sources is necessary to complete the task.
4. Dynamic model of differentiation (reading proficiency is a result of the interaction of readers with texts in particular situations; it is not a reader trait.
5. Guiding questions, essential questions, key questions, core/big understandings, and touchstone concepts are kept in the forefront of the class discussion.
6. Draw attention to puzzlements and conundrums, to things that puzzle us.
7. Gateway activities, hooks, or entry points for students to make meaningful connections.
8. Consequential tasks are meaningful to students and in the discipline.
9. Routines for metacognitive conversations.
10. Close reading of text to support engagement and reading carefully.
11. Support for text-based discussion citing evidence.
12. Argumentation templates to provide models for oral and written arguments.
13. Participation structures that provide opportunities for student talk.
14. Ongoing assessment and formative feedback.

We knew these were ill-defined—a good reflection of the messiness of our design conjectures at this point in the intervention development. Likewise, we had only vague and largely unstated assumptions about how these would mediate processes of learning and result in students developing core competencies. However, we expected to engage in reflections on how the implementations fared—what seemed to "work" for whom, what problems arose, what modifications teachers made while enacting the initial modules—and that these insights would be critical to revising our design and theoretical conjectures. As one principal investigator (PI) reminded the group, "We know we aren't going to get it right the first time."

Initial Evidence/Interpretation Charts in Science

The design and use of the E/I charts by the science team and in classrooms revealed the complexity of supporting EBA. Prior to introducing E/I charts in classrooms, science team members read and annotated two texts planned for the Water module and completed an E/I chart (Figure 6.1) to address the inquiry question: "How and where do we get fresh water?" The column headers in Figure 6.1 were intended to promote three processes: identification of text-based evidence; generation of claims, hypotheses, or questions; and reasoning between claims and evidence. Each team member was to complete the tasks individually and then share his or her ideas about how these potential texts and tasks fit with our existing core constructs and design features.

As members of the team shared their experiences and reactions, the complexity of what we were expecting of students became clear. A PI noted her struggle with the third column labeled *Implications: Claims, Hypotheses, Questions* (see Figure 6.1). She remarked that most of what she had written in that column appeared to be summary statements. "Are these really claims?" she wondered. Similarly, a research associate noted that filling out the E/I chart helped him discern important information from the text, but it did not seem to support him in constructing arguments: "It's a tool that should be a stimulus for students to need to make some sort of argument." Another PI countered by noting that making sense of the texts was a key step to engaging in text-based argument and that "you don't start by putting down evidence that's 'relevant' . . . it presupposes that [the students] know where they're going, because they don't know. Some of the

Inquiry	How and where do we get fresh water?		
Source (Reliability_ Data)	Data / Evidence / Excerpts	Implications Claims, hypotheses, questions	Making Thinking Visible
	What evidence is there for how and where we get fresh water?	What does the evidence suggest about how and where we get fresh water? What hypotheses are we forming? What questions do we have? What are the implications of the data?	How is the data or evidence related in your hypotheses of claims, in your view?

FIGURE 6.1   Preliminary E/I chart for Water module before classroom trials

things might be evidence, but not for the inquiry question we have." A former classroom teacher emphasized that the E/I chart should be "one step away from initial contact with the text" and treated as a more careful selection of aspects of the text that fit with the inquiry questions. Working through the texts and tasks as a team revealed different perspectives on the purpose and function of the E/I chart and pointed to differences in team members' conceptions of what counted as legitimate claims and evidence in the context of text-based inquiry.

This activity also made salient the inextricable relationship between the information selected for inclusion in the E/I charts, the texts, and the task. One research associate attributed the absence of claims to the inquiry question itself: "My hunch is that it has to do with the question itself. It's hard to get very interpretive about that [a how and where question]. Claims are about interpreting things." We could not resolve any of the tensions at this point, and a PI summarized this tension:

> The note taker(s) [E/I chart] and their role is a really interesting one. We need, but have not yet developed, a way to support students in making claims with the evidence and making explicit connections between them. It raises the question: how do we support claim making and the argument we want kids to get to?

Although these texts and tasks fit the criteria outlined in the core constructs and aligned with our design features, testing them revealed different perspectives about the purpose and function of each major component of the design (inquiry task/question, texts, and support charts) and interactions among them. This pushed our team to deeper consideration of how to begin supporting students' engagement with complex texts and the series of instructional scaffolds that would build their capacities to engage in EBA. We continued to wrestle with these questions as we began to conduct formative observations and collect artifacts as evidence of how teachers and students were engaging with inquiry questions, texts, and E/I charts. Our designs continued to evolve as we gained a better understanding of how various aspects supported students' engagement in text-based inquiry.

The experience of the science team was not unique. The history team had similar discussions about what made a piece of information evidence for a particular claim and whether sources produced at the time of a historical event were narratives that described what happened or should be regarded as claims that the event occurred. In the literature team, the discussions considered disciplinary disputes about the very nature of interpretive claims about a literary work.

Learning From Initial EBA Modules: The Inherent Messiness of Claims and Evidence

Over the course of a 2-day project-wide meeting at the end of the second year, there was lengthy discussion about the nature of claims and evidence in different text genres and the challenges this presented for creating tools to support students in differentiating them.

The science team reported on their experiences trying to use E/I charts to support the differentiation of claims and evidence. They shared that although students were learning to identify and interpret statements in the texts that would address the inquiry question, they were not yet distinguishing between claims and evidence in the text (Figure 6.2). For instance, students simultaneously listed statements that might be considered *claims* ("Bacteria can cause a disease") alongside statements that might be considered *evidence* ("The creek is contaminated"). Thus, despite the use of *evidence* as the column header in the E/I chart, students were not specifically distinguishing *claims* from *evidence*. Instead, they "treated both claims and evidence equally" (PI, meeting transcript).

One of the PIs on the science team noted that this lack of differentiation of claims and evidence should not be surprising given that most of the texts available in classrooms were textbooks: "This is what a science textbook does. It gives claim after claim after claim with no evidence for the claim." As a result, "it is sensible that students would see claims as evidence, when really they are to be treated quite differently, and it's clear that they don't know how to do that."

Although most members of the team agreed with this characterization of science textbooks, several PIs pointed out possible conceptual problems with teaching students to differentiate *claims* from *evidence*, writ large. One of the cognitive psychologists on the project pointed to the potential danger of conveying a false sense that the status of *claim* or *evidence* somehow inheres in any particular piece of information. She framed it this way:

> I'm just wondering if everything that is a claim can be evidence, and can also be a claim. [. . .] So you can use the same statement eventually to

SOURCE	Evidence (quotes from the text)	Interpretations (thoughts, connections, questions, etc.)
Tennessee Journalist: "Third Creek Unsafe for Swimming"	bacteria can cause a disease Found that Third Creek is contaminated *Sample response reads:* bacteria can cause a disease — Found that Third Creek is contaminated —	This bacteria is bad What exactly is this river contaminated with. *Sample response reads:* This bacteria is bad — What exactly is the river contaminated with.

FIGURE 6.2 Evidence/Interpretation chart for sixth grade Water module

support another statement, and it could need to be supported. So in a way it almost doesn't help I think [to focus on differentiating claims from evidence in a text]. I'm a reductionist, totally, and a component skills person, but this is the one piece I wouldn't reduce and teach people to distinguish these two things, because in the end, functionally, it's all the same. They have to use one piece of evidence to support another piece of evidence, which also has to be supported.

Another PI agreed: "Information in the abstract is not either claims or evidence. You can't generically distinguish. There's nothing inherent in the information that makes it a claim or evidence. It's its function in some context."

The impact of these exchanges on design decisions around E/I charts was messy; the goal for students to differentiate a claim from the evidence that supported it remained, but the design of the E/I charts shifted in the direction of distinguishing between information relevant and irrelevant to the inquiry question and being able to explain why it was relevant. For example, in the second iteration of the Water module, the E/I chart contained three column headers: (1) Evidence: What we saw in the text; (2) Interpretation: What we thought about it; and (3) Next Steps: What we think we know or need to know next (to address the inquiry question). This shift towards contextualizing the task in the inquiry question was similarly reflected in E/I chart design for the second iteration of the history modules. However, observations of student thinking led to additional adaptations to the support tools.

Expanding Supports Around E/I Charts: The Case of History

For the second iteration of the history modules, both the high school and middle school teachers started their classes by reorienting students to history as inquiry into the past, thereby motivating the interrogation of texts and other artifacts, repositioning them as potential sources of evidence about the past. A sixth grade teacher introduced the study of history by posing two questions—"What is history? How can we know about the past?"—and having students generate the kinds of questions historians might ask about artifacts from the past (Field notes, October 2, 2012). Students offered questions such as "What time period is this from?" and "What is the purpose of this object?" She then introduced an adapted version of the E/I chart with two columns labeled *Observations* and *Inferences*. Students used this to make observations and inferences about artifacts from the past (e.g., an antique rug beater, a catalogue of advertisements for a variety of rug beaters). During whole-class share-outs, the teacher used follow-up questions to elicit the reasoning for their inferences and modeled the targeted forms of reasoning.

During a meeting to debrief this lesson (October 2, 2012), the teacher and two history team researchers who had been participant observers during the lessons noted that sometimes students were differentiating observations from inferences but often they were not. For example, one student wrote about the catalogue: "On each picture it tells a couple of sentences of how its (sic) good to buy." The inference written next to this observation stated: "They are trying to persuade people to buy them." However, this same student also wrote in the observation column "A flyer that has pictures of carpet beaters" and in the corresponding inference column "It shows how 4 different designs of carpet beaters look like." The struggle to distinguish observations and inferences was pervasive among the students. As the teacher put it, "[students] get confused in the process" and tend to put their observations and inferences in "the wrong categories." She said she noticed that students tended to skip to making inferences without understanding how specific textual observations *led* to a given inference. One researcher observed "[students] don't slow their thinking enough to catch that that's now an inference." The other researcher reported

> that table [of students] was having trouble. Their observation was "it's cheap." Their inference was "it's cheap and useful." I was trying to get them to see you can't have it the same and how does cheap relate to useful. But they still seemed confused about that connection. They still thought cheap and they couldn't explain the connection.

The teacher and researchers engaged in productively messy brainstorming about additional ways of leading students to make their reasoning more explicit and thus better differentiate between observations and inferences. The teacher noted that she had previously used a three-column chart—observation, what I know, and inference—

> but I think that's even more confusing. You're breaking it down into the parts but you're being too obvious. Asking them to think about what they know so explicitly—it kind of confuses them. I like this [2 column chart] better but it leaves out a piece because you jump from observation to inference [leaving out the reasoning because there is no need to] write down what you know [that leads you to the inference].

She also did not think more modeling on her part was the answer: "They were dying, they wanted to say everything." As a result, the teacher reported that she did not think her efforts to model observations, inferences, and the reasoning from observation to inference were being heard. Ultimately, the tool introduced was sentence stems for observation statements and other stems for inference statements. Class discussions focused on the reasoning.

During the next history lesson (October 3, 2012), students brought in personal artifacts from their homes. They took turns making observations about each other's artifacts using sentence stems such as "I notice . . ." or "I see . . ."

or "I observe . . ." They then made inferences about each other's artifacts using sentence stems such as "I can infer . . ." or "I can guess . . ." or "I can figure out . . ." In debriefing this lesson, the teacher and researchers agreed that students were more successful at differentiating between observations and inferences and attributed this success to the sentence stems. As one researcher noted, "It's hard to say 'I notice this is special to your family' right? . . . You're not going to say, 'I can infer this is red.' So I thought that really scaffolded it." The differentiation was also evident in the statements written in the observation and inference columns of the charts. Thus, the teacher's design decision to make observations and inferences step by step with the support of sentence stems seemed to help students differentiate between the two processes.

The history teacher's design implementation illustrates the need for adaptations to be made in response to feedback that the support tools are not working for students. The "messiness" in the design-based research process is precisely the phenomena that Brown (1992) cited as motivating the need to engage in DBR in the first place. That is, the best-laid designs may turn out not to suit the particular context in which they are implemented for a variety of reasons, including the knowledge students bring to the task, as well as the affordances of the materials, tasks, and tools. This is a common phenomenon in instruction and one of the reasons teachers need to be adaptive experts (cf. Darling-Hammond & Bransford, 2007).

What Claims Are the E/I Charts Supposed to Support? The Case of Literature

Teachers on the literature team implemented modules that focused on the rhetorical device of symbolism in stories with a coming-of-age theme. However, they used different literary works, reflecting differences in grade levels (eighth, ninth, or eleventh) and student demographics. The literature E/I charts were intended to guide students in identifying and interpreting symbols in literary works (see Figure 6.3). The column headers directed students to reason from "What the text says" to "Associations I can make," and from these to "What the symbol means." This progression builds on textual evidence and both real-world and textual associations to determine the meaning of a symbol in a text, as understood by the student. However, this focus on simply what a symbol represents inside a text leads to what one PI, a former English teacher with a PhD in English education and the head of the literature design team, termed "symbol hunting." As she put it, without support to take it further, the message to students becomes "There (are these things) out there, symbols, they exist and you should know them, so go find them." Indeed, several teachers focused on "symbol hunting" in their initial attempts to enact symbolism modules, and once students identified and interpreted the symbols in a text, they left it at that. For instance, one of the teachers showed a video clip of two middle school students discussing the

Interpreting Symbolism			
What I think is symbolic: Image, event, character, action, object, name, places	What the text says (page #)	Assumptions I can make with the image, event, character, action, object, name, or place	What do the words in the text and the associations I make lead me to think about what the symbol means?

FIGURE 6.3 Literature E/I worksheet used to scaffold symbol identification and interpretation

meaning of the black cat in one of Edgar Allan Poe's stories. Literature team members noticed that although the students were discussing the meaning of the symbol, they never went beyond that to discuss the story. It appeared that from the students' perspectives, finding and interpreting the symbol was the end goal of the activity. The implementing teacher agreed and expressed the frustration of his students around the interpretation of the symbol on the E/I support sheet: "I don't get what [that] column is, I told you what it said in the text, I told you the associations I can make, and now I am just going to synthesize the second column and the third column (to put something in [it])." This reflected the problem with "symbol hunting": the students thought their task ended with the interpretation of the symbol.

This discussion of symbolic interpretation led to new insights about this process. As one member put it, once a reader has made an interpretation, he or she needs to think about how that interpretation relates to the text as a whole:

> The reasoning comes back to how much does that explain about what happened in the story and if you can create an argument about how much it explains then you have a reasonable argument and someone else can say it represents something else.

We began to understand that the ultimate argument was not about the meaning of the symbol, but rather how that meaning contributed to an overall understanding and interpretation of the text. This way of thinking about the E/I chart and the support that students needed led the teacher to a new understanding of the utility of the symbol column: "[H]ow much explanatory power does it give you, the so what, why do we care that you can make the associations about a black cat that they represent bad luck. Why does it matter in this text?" It became clear that the importance in doing activities with the symbolism E/I chart was in pushing students beyond the everyday understanding of the black cat symbolizing bad luck and getting them to think about why the author used a black cat and what it meant for the story.

In this meeting, the discussion stimulated by the video clips and the examination of the E/I chart exposed the raggedy nature of the team members' grasp of intended outcomes for symbolic interpretation. This was the case even though we had previously discussed how to support these interpretive processes. In our experiences, especially with multidisciplinary groups, key concepts frequently reflect this type of "messily" shared understanding. As in the present case, it often takes a joint activity engaged in by the group to reveal key differences that stimulate productive exploration of concepts fundamental to the group's work.

Discussion and Conclusions

The design story for each of the disciplinary teams did not begin with clear, coherent learning objectives for evidence-based argumentation. Instead, our design processes involved rounds of iteration and reflection by all members of the design teams based on observations of what happened during implementations and analyses of student work on the E/I charts. The iterative implementation and reflection moved our thinking toward clearer understandings about how specific design elements supported students in moving towards constructing explanatory and interpretive claims. This process is aptly described as "productively messy" in that we identified issues about which there was far from universal agreement or understanding among team members. These could not be easily or quickly resolved; design decisions were made in the midst of both uncertainty and urgency to test our imperfect designs in classrooms. Furthermore, we could not easily identify a single design or aspect of a designed artifact as the focal point of revision. Rather, we came to acknowledge the importance of aligning all components of our modules—the inquiry question, the E/I charts, and text sets—in order to move towards our objectives. Although messy, this process also resulted in productive advances, both to the designed artifacts and our own conceptions of how to support EBA in different disciplines.

Our description of this "productive messiness" differs from a typical depiction of the DBR process. Although we could have described how our design processes contribute to *ontological innovations* (diSessa & Cobb, 2004), we focused our efforts here on exposing the messy participatory design process that is often hidden in publications. It might be tempting to attribute the messiness to working in a large, interdisciplinary team. We argue, however, that part of the messiness reported here is a result of *not* iterating on existing tools (e.g., McNeill & Krajcik, 2009; Monte-Sano, De La Paz, & Felton, 2014) or attempting to use one argumentation design template across the disciplines. Instead, and consistent with design recommendations made by Smith, Smith, and Shen (2012), we started with analyses of disciplinary differences in conceptualizations of argument and students' existing competencies and dove into how teachers and students took up embodiments of our design conjectures. Our work suggests that DBR does not move in a linear, unidirectional fashion (cf. Figure 6.1, Sandoval, 2014), from conjectures to designed tools, and then to observed outcomes. Instead, studying the designed tools in action can reveal messiness that leads to greater clarity in theoretical conjectures about how these designs mediate desired outcomes.

Finally, our work suggests that the process of turning textual information into *evidence* for a *claim* is not straightforward. Supporting students in constructing arguments requires a critical examination of discipline-specific notions of argument that often go unexamined. Our work would have been severely limited if we had focused our efforts on making argument the *object* of teachers' and students' activity (Manz, 2014). Instead, we took up messy discussions and debates that clarified how argument serves as a *tool* for producing knowledge in each discipline. The three questions to which we have returned repeatedly throughout READI—"What is argument?" "What are similarities and differences based on discipline?" and "What instructional affordances support it and how?"—reflect our ongoing commitment to productive messiness. We speculate that these questions, and the subsequent disagreements, frustrations, and designs that resulted, would not have been so evident had our work been situated within a single discipline. In closing, we hope that this brief discussion of the participatory design process in READI provokes further conversations about the more designerly, messy, yet productive aspects of DBR.

Acknowledgments

This research was supported by the Institute of Education Sciences, U.S. Department of Education, through Grant R305F100007 to University of Illinois at Chicago in collaboration with Inquirium LLC, Northwestern University, Northern Illinois University, WestEd, and several large urban school districts. The opinions expressed are those of the authors and do not represent views of the institute or the U.S. Department of Education. The work discussed in this chapter was conducted in collaboration with Project READI members Stephen Briner, M. Ann Britt, Willard Brown, Candice Burkett, Irisa Charney-Sirott, Rick Coppola, Jessica Chambers, Gayle Cribb, Cynthia Greenleaf, Thomas Griffin, Jenny Gustavson, Gina Hale, Jodi Hoard, Johanna Heppler, Adriana Jaureguy, Kimberly Lawless, Carol D. Lee, Rachel Letizia, Sarah Levine, Cindy Litman, Joseph Magliano, Michael Manderino, Stacy Marple, Kathryn McCarthy, Katie McIntyre, Courtney Milligan, James W. Pellegrino, Diane Puklin, Cynthia Shanahan, Tanya Solomon, Teresa Sosa, Patty Wallace, Jennifer Wiley, and Mariya Yukhymenko.

References

Archer, L.B. (1979). Whatever became of design methodology? *Design Studies, 1*(1), 17–20.

Barab, S., Zuiker, S., Warren, S., Hickey, D., Ingram-Goble, A., Kwon, E.J., . . . Herring, S.C. (2007). Situationally embodied curriculum: Relating formalisms and contexts. *Science Education, 91*(5), 750–782.

Bransford, JD., Brown, A.L., & Cocking, R.R. (2000). *How people learn: Brain, mind, experience, and school.* Washington, DC: National Academy of Sciences.

Britt, M.A., & Aglinskas, C. (2002). Improving students' ability to identify and use source information. *Cognition and Instruction, 20*(4), 485–522.

Brown, A.L. (1992). Design experiments: Theoretical and methodological challenges in creating complex interventions in classroom settings. *Journal of the Learning Sciences, 2*(2), 141–178. doi:10.1207/s15327809jls0202_2.

Cross, N. (2007). Forty years of design research. *Design Studies, 28*(1), 1–4.

Darling-Hammond, L., & Bransford, J. (2007). *Preparing teachers for a changing world: What teachers should learn and be able to do.* San Francisco, CA: Jossey-Bass.

diSessa, A.A., & Cobb, P. (2004). Ontological innovation and the role of theory in design experiments. *The Journal of the Learning Sciences, 13*(1), 77–103. doi:10.1207/s15327809jls1301_4.

Donovan, M.S., & Bransford, J. (2005). *How students learn: History, mathematics, and science in the classroom.* Washington, DC: National Academy Press.

Gee, J.P. (1992). *The social mind: Language, ideology, and social practice.* New York, NY: Bergin & Garvey.

Goldman, S.R. (2012). Adolescent literacy: Learning and understanding content. *Future of Children, 22*(2), 89–116.

Goldman, S.R., & Bisanz, G.L. (2002). Toward a functional analysis of scientific genres: Implications for understanding and learning processes. In J. Otero, J.A. León, & A.C. Graesser (Eds.), *The psychology of science text comprehension* (pp. 19–50). Mahwah, NJ: Erlbaum.

Goldman, S.R., Braasch, J.L., Wiley, J., Graesser, A.C., & Brodowinska, K. (2012). Comprehending and learning from Internet sources: Processing patterns of better and poorer learners. *Reading Research Quarterly, 47*(4), 356–381.

Goldman, S.R., Britt, M.A., Brown, W., Cribb, G., George, M., Greenleaf, C., Lee, C.D., & Shanahan, C. (submitted). A conceptual framework for disciplinary literacy. *Educational Psychologist.*

Lee, C.D. (2007). *Culture, literacy, and learning.* New York, NY: Teachers College Press.

Lee, C.D., & Spratley, A. (2010). *Reading in the disciplines: The challenges of adolescent literacy.* New York, NY: Carnegie Corporation of New York.

Manz, E. (2014). Representing student argumentation as functionally emergent from scientific activity. *Review of Educational Research.* doi:10.3102/0034654314558490.

McNeill, K.L., & Krajcik, J. (2009). Synergy between teacher practices and curricular scaffolds to support students in using domain-specific and domain-general knowledge in writing arguments to explain phenomena. *Journal of the Learning Sciences, 18*(3), 416–460.

Monte-Sano, C., De La Paz, S., & Felton, M. (2014). *Reading, thinking, and writing about history.* New York, NY: Teachers College Press.

New London Group. (1996). A pedagogy of multiliteracies: Designing social futures. *Harvard Educational Review, 66*(1), 60–92.

Radinsky, J., Loh, B., & Lukasik, J. (2008). *GIS tools for historical inquiry: Issues for classroom-centered design*: Ann Arbor, MI: MPublishing, University of Michigan Library.

Sandoval, W. (2014). Conjecture mapping: An approach to systematic educational design research. *Journal of the Learning Sciences, 23*(1), 18–36. doi:10.1080/10508406.2013.778204.

Schoenbach, R., Greenleaf, C., & Murphy, L. (2012). *Reading for understanding: How reading apprenticeship improves disciplinary learning in secondary and college classroom.* San Francisco, CA: Jossey-Bass.

Shanahan, T., & Shanahan, C. (2008). Teaching disciplinary literacy to adolescents: Rethinking content-area literacy. *Harvard Educational Review, 78*(1), 40–59.

Smith, S., Smith, G., & Shen, Y.-T. (2012). Redesign for product innovation. *Design Studies, 33*(2), 160–184.

The Design-Based Research Collective. (2003). Design-based research: An emerging paradigm for educational inquiry. *Educational Researcher, 32*(1), 5–8. doi:10.3102/0013189X032001005.

Toulmin, S., Rieke, R., & Janik, A. (1984). *An introduction to reasoning.* New York, NY: Macmillan.

Voogt, J., Laferrière, T., Breuleux, A., Itow, R.C., Hickey, D.T., & McKenney, S. (2015). Collaborative design as a form of professional development. *Instructional Science, 43*(2), 259–282.

Wiley, J., & Voss, J.F. (1999). Constructing arguments from multiple sources: Tasks that promote understanding and not just memory for text. *Journal of Educational Psychology, 91*(2), 301.

7

RECIPROCAL RESEARCH AND DESIGN

The Wicked Problem of Changing Math in the Family

Shelley Goldman and Osvaldo Jiménez

Introduction

Rittel and Webber (1973) characterized design and planning problems as "wicked" for a variety of reasons, such as for being complex, for being difficult to describe and define, and for not presenting or prescribing optimal solutions. The wicked depiction was partially to distinguish complex design problems from the kinds of problems taken up by science and engineering (Cross, 2007). Wicked problems often go unsolved and stand in contrast to problems that are "tame," such as a math problem or puzzle to be solved. Much debate in the design literature has taken place around this idea of wicked problems. The wickedness of design problems has been described as helping designers move away from linear thinking about the design process and forcing them to take an active role in defining and shaping the design problem to be solved (Buchanan, 1992). Cross (2007) suggests that Rittel's wicked depiction also opened space for the generation of innovative design methods that engage the designer with more participatory practices and partnering with the problem owners.

We use these notions of wicked problems in our work on research and design concerning families and how they seize opportunities for enacting, learning, and increasing the amount of math they encounter in their daily lives (Esmonde et al., 2012; Goldman, Martin, Pea, Booker, & Blair, 2006). Based on our research, we have learned that anyone designing experiences for math engagement in the family is trying to solve a wicked problem. Math itself is considered difficult by many, and with its gatekeeping tendencies as a school subject, it also generates a great deal of anxiety and avoidance for people (Boaler, 2012; Goldman, 2005). Designing ways to engage adults and children in math can truly be a wicked problem where design solutions are not obvious or guaranteed. Also, we knew we would learn more about the family math problem space through the design process, but felt confident that we would learn enough through the process to design solutions that were responsive to the math needs of the families.

Our approach for addressing the wicked problem of how to open up more opportunities for families to use and enjoy math was to engage in a design process that draws on prior research about math engagements, but also stays close to the families with an empathy-driven, user-centered approach. We hoped this approach, reciprocal research and design (RR&D), would result in deeper understandings about how families interact with math *and* how to design math environments for families that would increase their math exposure (Alexander et al., 2010). Herein, we chronicle and critique aspects of the RR&D design process employed to better understand where it was essential to developing our understanding of the problem space and what it contributed in terms of design solutions aimed at our wicked problem of family math. We proceed by describing and critiquing the RR&D process and reporting on the complex and somewhat unexpected findings we uncovered in the design of mobile math learning apps for families with children in grades 4 to 8 (ages 9 to 11).

The process cycled through applying basic research findings about how families engaged mathematical problem solving, to designing the applications that could seed those types of math more broadly, to researching the impact of the designs. The basic research findings came from interview research we conducted about math learning in families that had no design aspect or specified end goal in mind. The design constraints we applied throughout the process, the math content we covered in our designs, and the game-like "fun" factors evolved from the basic research findings. For example, the choice to develop mobile applications came from what we learned about families on the go and their growing access to mobile technologies. The basic research enabled us to develop empathy for the families who might be our users. We coalesced these findings into ideas for family math application designs. Once we had prototypes, we moved to further develop, test, and iterate through "ride along" user studies. After several rounds of iterations and many revisions, we put a suite of five mini-games collectively called *Go RoadTrip!* to the test in a second basic research project with 30 families. This last research round was a hybrid. It was structured a lot like a basic research study, but was also meant to direct the next phases of design and development. The rounds of the RR&D process enabled us to create family math environments while also helping us learn more about math in families.

The results were mixed, with only partial success being reported. The *Go RoadTrip!* apps were enjoyed by the middle school participants and changed their ideas of what constitutes "math." On the positive side, the middle school participants preferred practicing math in the apps to doing so on homework. However, the apps did not achieve the intended effects of increasing social interaction around math in the families at any level of significance, and we learned that there is some reconceptualizing of platform and social engineering needed in the next design round. Based on these results, we will discuss the RR&D process and the results associated with each step, and use the process to highlight and reflect on how it has helped inform our future process and ideas on addressing wicked problems in the learning sciences.

The RR&D Process

The RR&D research and user-centered methods find their roots in design traditions and design studies (Cross, 2007). RR&D practices are closely aligned with the participatory design movement, human–computer interface studies in computer science, design thinking, and design-based research in the learning sciences (Asaro, 2000; Brown, 1992; Ehn, 1992) and draw on an array of methods, processes, and orientations for involving multiple stakeholders and end users in the design process (Asaro, 2000; Goldman, Mercier, & Booker, 2009; Roschelle & DiGiano, 2004). The field of design thinking contributes greatly with its commitment to empathy-driven, human-centered design in pursuit of designing complex problem solutions (Kelley, 2001). The idea of combining research and design has taken hold in the learning sciences at the intersections of research, classroom, curriculum and assessment, and technology design (Barab, Thomas, Dodge, Squire, & Newell, 2004; Brown, 1992; Edelson, Gordin, & Pea, 1999; Goldman et al., 2009; Hmelo, Holton, & Kolodner, 2000; Penuel, Roschelle, & Shechtman, 2007; Peppler & Glosson, 2013).

The RR&D process has a reflexive and reciprocal relationship with basic research, user-based studies, and learning designs (Alexander et al., 2010). The impetus and blueprints for family math originated in findings from a basic research study about math in families (Esmonde et al., 2012; Goldman et al., 2006). The approach was meant to balance the voice of our participants, the affordances of emerging technologies such as the mobile platform (Rogers & Price, 2009; Roschelle, 2003), and familial strategies for engaging learners. We see the RR&D process driving the design and development to a "third space" in technology (Muller, 2002) and learning development (Gutierrez, Baquedano-López, & Tejeda, 1999). Third space is a synergistic space for imagining new ideas and solutions—a space for vision that comes from multiple perspectives where dominant and nondominant factors or positions all have equal sway, making hybrid solutions possible. We see it as the design concept space where the reflective and reflexive nature of the RR&D process comes to fruition. In our case, it is the nexus for negotiating and achieving insights about the mobile platform's affordances and constraints, what we know about family math practices, and how the mobile apps might interface with the institutional and cultural settings of their use.

Applying the RR&D Process

We analyze and critique the RR&D process in the following ways. First, we highlight the findings of our initial interview study that had implications for the *Go Math!* development and research process and show how they determined design constraints for the development efforts. Second, we illustrate the reciprocal and generative nature of the design process through examples from the applications and user studies. Third, we explain how, with a version of the apps in hand, we moved to a hands-off research study to see what we could learn about how families treat math games and better understand their potential in comparison to more typical ways to practice math.

The Basic Research

In our initial basic research, we interviewed 24 families, videotaping the interviews and a math-related task that we gave them, identifying the many mathematical problem-solving activities in which they engaged (Goldman et al., 2006). When we embarked on the research, we sought to identify the contexts, activities, and resources brought to bear on learning mathematics in families. Throughout data analysis, we strove to keep the first person voices of our participants, and whether we were conducting quantitative or qualitative analyses, we continually returned to our primary video recordings of the interviews and family activities to keep our design decisions aligned with our understandings about the needs of our family participants.

Research results and direct instances from the initial interviews themselves were repeatedly extracted and examined to inform design decisions. Three areas of findings from our initial study anchored the mobile design: (1) features of family problem solving; (2) the participatory nature of mathematics activities; and (3) differences between math at home and math at school. We discuss each briefly.

Math problems evolved as families dealt with daily demands. The problems could be extremely complex given the situated and contextual nature of life problems. Problems were taken up when the family placed value on solving them (Pea & Martin, 2010). Some examples were budgeting, home improvements, and planning celebrations.

Problem solving in the family was often a social engagement. Collaborations came about because one family member held some relevant expertise, such as when a child asked the parent to help with a problem or a parent felt that it would be good for a child to help out with something related to their school math, such as calculating a tip at a restaurant.

We found several distinctions between how people depicted math at home and math at school (Esmonde et al., 2012). Stories of school math were about mathematics as an end in itself; the problem-solving methods, conventions, and tools were specified, and evaluation was externally bestowed. In contrast, family math stories were about addressing local concerns. They included supporting personal and social goals such as playing games, staying on budget, making charitable donations, or teaching financial responsibility (Martin & Goldman,

2010). Families made use of both conventional and unconventional methods and resources, and their math work and resulting solutions were often evaluated in situ.

From Research to Design Ideation and Development

We based our design decisions on the basic research findings, user feedback throughout the development phases, and software platform and development considerations. Our goal was to design environments to support more interaction with math in families. We saw families enjoy math together and learned about the conditions that brought about these math-related engagements. The research results indicated that it would be beneficial to help families accomplish math while they were on the go and at home together. Two examples stand out. Time in the car seemed like family time ripe for some math fun. We also had data from the basic research showing us how excited and involved the families were when they worked on a task that involved cell phone service packages during the interviews. These two insights led to the decision to develop mobile applications to address the emerging design problem.

The translation from research findings to design considerations and development engaged the team in a series of specific steps and activities that started with interrogating the research, to developing deep empathy for the families, to third-space brainstorming, to working on functionality and features, to cycling through user testing and revisions, and finally to a second research study.

The research helped us develop design specifications—a set of needs and constraints we attended to in our designing. These were that the environments needed to:

1. Be situation-driven
2. Promote enjoyment of mathematics
3. Demonstrate the value of mathematizing experience by helping parents and kids discover the math in everyday situations and contexts
4. Be driven by values (if people do not see it as an important problem, they will not engage it)
5. Reinforce the family as a social unit of mathematical activity and learning
6. Be a complement to school: math activities in the applications are complementary and supportive of school math up to first-year algebra
7. Take advantage of technology affordances.

We focused *Go RoadTrip!* technology development on mobile devices because we knew from our research that families used mobiles everywhere, which creates opportunities for math while on the go. The other design specifications were also kept in mind as we tried to highlight their presence in the different mobile apps that were created. This led us to identify a set of questions that we discussed regularly, like whether the application was making familial–community–school links possible or whether the application was encouraging or promoting peer-based or intergenerational conversations (Alexander et al., 2010).

From Ideation to Math App Development

We moved to developing math technology environments for families. We chose to design web-based mobile applications for a variety of reasons, but central to our decision was our desire to reach the widest number of devices with limited resources. Mobiles were on their way to becoming a ubiquitous platform and powerful tools for learning (Rogers & Price, 2009; Roschelle, 2003). They had the advantage of integrating disparate consumer devices such as cameras, music players, video recorders, gaming, phones, e-mails, and browsers. They also enabled us to fulfill the on-the-go imperative that was clearly a big part of family time.

After brainstorming and storyboarding possible applications, we developed paper-based prototypes for each and tested them with new users. We were immediately faced with trade-offs that put our design specifications in conflict. One difficult decision we had to make was how to support one of our priority specifications—social activities—within the apps. We considered whether the application's social activities would require each user to have his or her own phone or create a shared experience around a single phone. We made a decision to design a single shared experience after determining the 2007 to 2008 state of mobile usage in our interview families and the general marketplace, the children's access to mobiles, what we learned from preliminary storyboard phase feedback, and financial estimates for development. Priority for a single shared math experience was given to the fact that most of fourth through seventh grade children did not have access to their own smartphones during the development period.

The *Go RoadTrip!* app was inspired by the kinds of games families told us they played in the car and what we learned of math in families. Keeping in line with our design specifications and questions, the games were meant to reinforce the family as a social unit by having both peer-based and intergenerational components, to help families discover math in everyday situations, to promote enjoyment of math, to involve competitive and collaborative problem-solving opportunities, and to correspond with school math topics.

The resulting *Go RoadTrip!* suite included five mini-games. These included logic games, word problems and puzzles, number pattern and sense games, an estimation game (e.g., how many silver cars will you see in 3 minutes), and a trip time/distance estimator game. No one game in the suite instantiated all of the design specifications, but they came close as a group. They put math fun into the hands of family members and addressed school math topics without rehashing them. They were designed to be mathematically engaging, aesthetically pleasing, and game-like (Figure 7.1). Children chose their own avatars, amassed points, and were given "cool" cars as they accumulated higher scores.

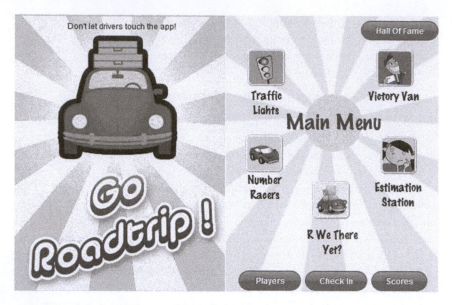

FIGURE 7.1   Initial game screen (left) and main games (right) in *Go RoadTrip!*

Two examples show the match to design specifications. *Traffic Lights* was modeled after *Mastermind*; either a player chooses a secret three-digit number or one is randomly generated. Then the remaining players guessed a three-digit number and received feedback: a red light indicated that a chosen digit did not appear in the secret number; a yellow light indicated that the number was correct but in the wrong place; and a green light indicated the number was both correct and in the correct place (see Figure 7.2). The game was designed to instigate conversation and collaboration among players for solving the secret number in the fewest number of guesses.

Another game, *Victory Van*, was a trivia game modeled after the *Cash Cab* television trivia game. Players first chose a fixed amount of time and then took turns answering questions until the preselected time ran out. We created 500+ multiple choice and free response questions that related to school math standards, such as the following sample problem (see Figure 7.3).

We performed a series of user studies and engaged in revision processes with three families over a period of several months. The user tests did not simply place a designed app in front of parents and children in an out-of-context situation and ask for their feedback. We put families in on-the-go situations, such as an extended car ride where they played with the prototype while we "rode along," observing, questioning, and videotaping. The family members were interviewed at the conclusion of the ride-along. We also collected back-end data to keep track of the family members' in-game activity. In all three cases, family members passed the phone during play and had discussions around the app and

FIGURE 7.2 Feedback on a guess (left) and the previous guess history (right) in *Traffic Lights*

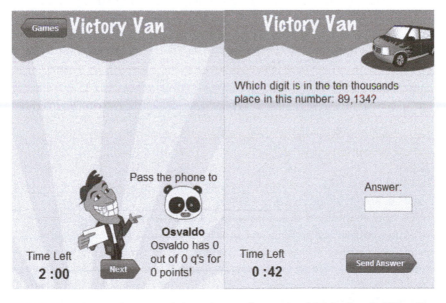

FIGURE 7.3 The initial prompt (left) and a sample question (right) given in *Victory Van*

its activities. We learned how the children and adults handled interface design issues, we saw if the math interactions were calibrated to children's skills and competencies, and we got suggestions for ways to heighten enjoyment.

In one field test, two brothers were playing *Traffic Lights* and through repeated play and discussion, discovered a mistake in the game's logic structure. They realized that if they chose a three-digit number with a repeating digit (i.e., 222), the app could not respond with proper feedback. In another field test, we discovered that we had to let the family decide how much time should be allotted for solving and answering the problems they encountered. From a third family, we learned that the children wanted the apps to be more gamified, meaning that they expected a reward system. Based on analyzing each ride-along, we iterated the design towards a more useful, fun suite of apps that would meet our emerging design goals. Once we thought the apps were ready for a larger number of families to use, we placed the apps at the center of the next round of research aimed at understanding whether playing *Go RoadTrip!* enhanced mathematical interaction in families.

Results of the RR&D Second Round of Research

Design processes often move iteratively between cycles of design and testing. In our work, we felt that we reached the place where user testing with families and prioritized fixes were not necessarily giving us new development directions. To see if we achieved our aims and to know whether it was time to invest more heavily in the development of the applications, it was important to complete an additional round of research. We wanted to know if *Go RoadTrip!* was achieving its social, enjoyment, and math engagement goals. Using a comparative research study design, we enrolled children in grades 4 to 8 and at least one parent in each family in one of two conditions: a mobile game condition or a math homework condition. We required each participating family to have some form of smartphone with 3G capability in order to create an equitable sample, although assignments to the conditions were random. We enrolled 63 children (26 males, 34 females) in grades 4 to 7, with one eighth grader included in the sample. Forty-six parents of the children enrolled.

The game condition included using *Go RoadTrip!*. The homework condition included solving problem worksheets online that generated equivalent/comparable math problems to those that appeared in the games. As part of the study, children took math assessments before and after the study, spent time in the environments, and were asked (along with their parents) to fill out attitudinal surveys. We also interviewed six of the families after they finished their participation using a semi-structured interview protocol to watch families complete the tasks in their conditions and learn how they viewed their experiences.

The comparison condition enabled us to create a condition that provided students with the same mathematical content but not in a game-like manner.

Although we initially thought that we would simply do a paper-and-pencil type set of worksheets (hence why we dubbed it the "homework condition" and the *Go RoadTrip!* games the "game condition"), the project involved using cell phone technology, so we decided to create a comparable digital condition. Students could select from four types of worksheets—Calculations, Probability and Statistics, Number Properties, and Algebra and Geometry—and were then presented with 15 math problems to solve. For example, the homework condition used the same 500+ math problems as *Victory Van* in the game condition, but they were presented in a more traditional form. After students submitted their answers, they were able to view their corrected forms the following day.

Students in both conditions were asked to play a total of 2 hours of over a 7- to 14-day period. Progress was monitored by the research team via back-end data. Once 2 hours had been reached, children and parents were asked to complete post-attitudinal surveys and children were asked to complete a post-math assessment. Thirty-five children, 60% in the game condition and 57% in the homework condition, finished the study. When there was a dropout, parents most often described it as related to extreme schedule management, school pressures, or frustrations that the apps were not working fast or correctly (web apps were slower than stand-alone apps, especially when they were accessed over cellular networks and were not as polished as those commercially available).

Analysis of students' pre-attitudinal surveys showed that the two randomly created groups were similar in important ways. Overall, the self-reported data from the sample was heavily biased toward enjoyment and being good at math. In addition, students overwhelmingly reported that being good at math was clearly important to them and their families. The students showed a strong growth mind-set (Dweck, 2006) toward math, believing that effort rather than innate ability contributes toward success in math. There was initial disagreement as to whether math was a more procedural than conceptual subject, with approximately one-third of the students in each condition feeling that math is more procedural. In the post-attitudinal surveys, however, and in both conditions, students overwhelmingly felt that math was more conceptual. This may be related to the kinds of problems and the problem contexts we created.

Another important commonality amongst both groups was a strong feeling that math was a solitary activity. In both conditions, both pre- and post-attitudinal surveys strongly showed a bias toward preferring to do math alone. Both groups similarly reported that doing math alone was easier than working with others, with the post-attitude surveys confirming this feeling.

The post-attitudinal survey asked students to reflect on their experience with the math in both conditions, and overall the results were fairly similar. When asked if they had fun with this activity, students reported slightly more enjoyment in the game condition than in the homework condition, but overall students felt mostly neutral. Although both groups also felt that these activities were different from the math they do at school, students strongly preferred the game condition to the homework condition in terms of what they would prefer their homework to look like. So even though the participants enjoyed both conditions, it appears that the game condition was preferred.

These results were confounded by the fact that the children and families co-opted the homework and game conditions by incorporating them into their family practices. Although the game condition was specifically designed to be played in the car or on the go, with games such as *R We There Yet?* and *Estimation Station* meant to be played in a moving car, 24% of the children in the apps group reported that they never once played in the car, and only 65% reported playing in the car up to two times. We saw the corollary take place in the homework condition, which was initially not intended to be mobile at all, yet 33% of the children reported playing the homework condition in the car at least once, thereby mobilizing the nonmobile condition.

Discussion and Summary

The RR&D process in *Go RoadTrip!* produced unanticipated results that moved us beyond our typical user studies in designing for the wicked problem space of family math. First, the RR&D process kept us closely aligned with families and helped us develop some ideals for what we see as feasible for the family math space. We drew our design inspiration from what we learned from the families. One family told us of how they played games in the car, and the games they described became the inspiration for one of the apps. The process catalyzed development work and was important for understanding how mobile platforms could support and enhance math engagement in families. It enabled us to experiment with insights about how to integrate people, platforms, and new kinds of social arrangements. It added rigor to our process and helped us take chances in the design.

Our work was situated in a university setting, and it is not incidental that we had an imperative to complete both basic research and a comparative study. The RR&D process had the benefit of creating links between the theory-building work we do in learning research while keeping us involved with and contributing to the lives of families. We are pleased that we have been able to engage in a process that enables us to manage our professional missions while maintaining the spirit of empathy-driven design processes.

In retrospect, the process also had its limitations. We came to believe that we had more of an effect on increasing opportunities for socially involved math than we actually did. Our second research study showed that simply putting mobile apps in people's hands was not enough to change their behaviors, especially since we could not directly influence how they use the technology. One explanation for this is that we may have experienced a bit of an experimenter effect when we field-tested *Go RoadTrip!* When we were present and had the resources for social math in hand, the family members participated as a social unit. Yet, when we left the math games in the hands of the family with unstructured and unscripted instructions, the children resorted to individual game play. In essence, we, the experimenters, affected how the families used the apps. The second round of research uncovered some new insights into the role of math in the mix of everyday family life activities. Through interviewing six of the families in the second study, we learned that families had so many competing demands that parents thought it best to let the children take the apps and play with them while they were doing other daily tasks. The social experiences with math that we uncovered in our initial interview study did not carry forward when families were not setting aside special family time to meet with us. Therefore, this is a cautionary tale for those practicing user-centered design that includes human–computer interface design and field testing. We found that it was difficult to disrupt individual mind-sets around math and replace them with our vision of socially engaged math and to think that a mobile app would dictate the conditions of how, when, and where people will use it.

The process—although not totally consistent with typical design practices—helped us understand how much of a challenge it would be to design for the wicked problem of bringing more social versions of math into families. We find that the surfacing of these design shortcomings is consistent with RR&D. We expect design to be a process of iteration, and we can imagine the next step being a new round of design and user studies where we try to make the social aspects of the game more salient, compelling, and easy for the family members to access. Or do we let these goals go?

We recognize that a lengthy and complex RR&D process is not a realistic goal for every design process. We generated value through connecting basic research forays with our user-centered design process. This chapter demonstrates how an RR&D model is possible and has value in design. As noted earlier, we see other design-based researchers in the learning sciences relying on basic studies as part of their development projects. In terms of design scholarship, RR&D has helped us to deeply know our users, ideate about our potential designs, generate design criteria, and deal with trade-offs in a confident way while learning more about how to address the wicked problem of bringing more socially engaged math into families.

Acknowledgments

We are grateful to Roy Pea and all other members of the Family Math team at Stanford University and to the families who worked with us. This work was supported by the LIFE Center, NSF Grant No. 0354453. Any opinions, findings, and conclusions or recommendations expressed in this material are those of the author(s) and do not necessarily reflect the views of the National Science Foundation.

References

Alexander, A., Blair, K.P., Goldman, S., Jiménez, O., Nakaue, M., Pea, R., & Russell, A. (2010). Go Math! How research anchors new mobile learning environments. *2010 6th IEEE international conference on Wireless, Mobile and Ubiquitous Technologies in Education (WMUTE)* (pp. 57–64). Taiwan: Kaohsiung.

Asaro, P.M. (2000). Transforming society by transforming technology: The science and politics of participatory design. *Accounting, Management and Information Technologies, 10*(4), 257–290.

Barab, S.A., Thomas, M.K., Dodge, T., Squire, K., & Newell, M. (2004). Critical design ethnography: Designing for change. *Anthropology & Education Quarterly, 35*(2), 254–268.

Boaler, J. (2012). Timed tests and the development of math anxiety. *Education Week*, 1–3.

Brown, A.L. (1992). Design experiments: Theoretical and methodological challenges in creating complex interventions in classroom settings. *The Journal of the Learning Sciences, 2*(2), 141–178.

Buchanan, R. (1992). Wicked problems in design thinking. *Design Issues, 8*(2), 5–21.

Cross, N. (2007). Forty years of design research. *Design Studies, 28*(1), 1–4.

Dweck, C. (2006). *Mindset: The new psychology of success.* New York, NY: Random House.

Edelson, D.C., Gordin, D.N., & Pea, R.D. (1999). Addressing the challenges of inquiry-based learning through technology and curriculum design. *Journal of the Learning Sciences, 8*(3–4), 391–450.

Ehn, P. (1992). Scandinavian design: On participation and skill. In P.S. Adler & T.A. Winograd (Eds.), *Usability: Turning technologies into tools* (pp. 96–132). New York: Oxford University Press.

Esmonde, I., Blair, K.P., Goldman, S., Martin, L., Jiménez, O., & Pea, R. (2012). Math I am: What we learn from stories that people tell about math in their lives. In B. Bevan, P. Bell, R. Stevens, & A. Razfar (Eds.), *LOST opportunities: Learning in out-of-school time* (pp. 7–27). New York, NY: Springer.

Goldman, S. (2005). A new angle on families: Connecting the mathematics in daily life with school mathematics. In Z. Bekerman, N. Burbules, & D. Silberman-Keller (Eds.), *Learning in places: The informal education reader* (pp. 55–76). Bern, Switzerland: Peter Lang Publishing Group.

Goldman, S., Martin, L., Pea, R., Booker, A., & Blair, K. (2006). Problem emergence, problem solving, and mathematics in family life. In *Proceedings of the 7th international conference of the learning sciences* (pp. 1088–1093). Bloomington, IN: ISLS.

Goldman, S., Mercier, E., & Booker, A. (2009). Partnering with K-12 educators in collaborative design of learning technology. In C. DiGiano, S. Goldman, & M. Chorost (Eds.), *Educating learning technology designers* (pp. 62–79). New York, NY: Routledge.

Gutierrez, K.D., Baquedano-López, P., & Tejeda, C. (1999). Rethinking diversity: Hybridity and hybrid language practices in the third space. *Mind, Culture, and Activity, 6*(4), 286–303.

Hmelo, C.E., Holton, D.L., & Kolodner, J.L. (2000). Designing to learn about complex systems. *The Journal of the Learning Sciences, 9*(3), 247–298.

Kelley, T. (2001). *The art of innovation: Lessons in creativity from IDEO, America's leading design firm.* New York, NY: Doubleday.

Martin, L., & Goldman, S. (2010). Family inheritance: Parallel practices of financial responsibility in families. In L. Lin, H. Varenne, & E. Gordon (Eds.), *Educating comprehensively: Varieties of educational experiences, Vol. 3 of the Perspectives on comprehensive education series* (pp. 257–280). Lewiston, NY: The Edward Mellen Press.

8

DESIGNING THE CONNECTED CHEMISTRY CURRICULUM

Mike Stieff and Stephanie Ryan

Introduction

The *Connected Chemistry Curriculum Project* (Stieff, Nighelli, Yip, Ryan, & Berry, 2012) is a design-based research project that involves the iterative development and study of a technology-infused curriculum for supporting chemistry learning. The *Connected Chemistry Curriculum* (CCC) makes use of visualization software to improve conceptual understanding and representational competence in secondary chemistry (Gilbert, 2005). To accomplish this, CCC employs visualization software that includes visual representations embedded in a modeling environment as the core component of most learning activities. CCC began as several short, self-contained inquiry lessons (Levy & Wilensky, 2009a, 2009b; Stieff, 2011a; Stieff & Wilensky, 2003), and it has evolved into a comprehensive modular curriculum spanning approximately 120 hours of instruction. A diverse group of teachers, students, scientists, and design-based researchers have developed and studied the curriculum to produce a software suite, a set of curriculum artifacts, and complementary teacher guides used by school districts in 35 U.S. states and eight countries worldwide.

In this chapter we recount the CCC design process by which we organized our workflow and managed human resources. We avoid discussing student learning process and outcome studies of the curriculum, as those results have been documented elsewhere (cf., 2003; Ryan, Yip, Stieff, & Druin, 2013; Stieff, 2005, 2011a, 2011b; Stieff & McCombs, 2006). We highlight three challenges the design team faced while creating CCC. Specifically, we discuss challenges building and sustaining a collaborative design team, resolving conflicts between design aspirations and available resources, and conducting curriculum development in live classrooms. It is not our goal to provide prescriptive solutions to

Muller, M.J. (2002). Participatory design: The third space in HCI. In J.A. Jacko & A. Sears (Eds.). *Human-computer interaction handbook: Fundamentals, evolving techniques and emerging applications* (pp. 1051–1068). Mahwah, NJ: Lawrence Erlbaum.

Pea, R., & Martin, L. (2010). Values that occasion and guide mathematics in the family. In K. O'Connor & W.R. Penuel (Eds.), *Research on learning as a human science* (pp. 34–52). New York: Teachers College Press.

Penuel, W.R., Roschelle, J., & Shechtman, N. (2007). Designing formative assessment software with teachers: An analysis of the co-design process. *Research and Practice in Technology Enhanced Learning, 2*(1), 51–74.

Peppler, K., & Glosson, D. (2013). Stitching circuits: Learning about circuitry through e-textile materials. *Journal of Science Education and Technology, 22*(5), 751–763.

Rittel, H.W.J., & Webber, M.M. (1973). Dilemmas in a general theory of planning. *Policy Sciences, 4*(2), 155–169.

Rogers, Y., & Price, S. (2009). How mobile technologies are changing the way children learn. In A. Druin (Ed.), *Mobile technology for children: Designing for interaction and learning* (pp. 3–22). Boston, MA: Morgan Kaufmann.

Roschelle, J. (2003). Unlocking the learning value of wireless mobile devices. *Journal of Computer Assisted Learning, 19*(3), 260–272.

Roschelle, J., & DiGiano, C. (2004). ESCOT: Coordinating the influence of R&D and classroom practice to produce educational software from reusable components. *Interactive Learning Environments, 12*(1–2), 73–107.

each of these challenges. Rather, we will discuss how our team addressed each challenge and how our approach resolved or mitigated the issues.

The Connected Chemistry Curriculum

We designed CCC to address several perceived needs expressed by teachers, students, and scholars studying chemistry teaching and learning. Specifically, the curriculum was developed to help chemistry students connect their observations from the visible macroscopic world to the invisible submicroscopic world (Johnstone, 1993). Chemistry students often express difficulty coordinating their understanding of microscopic and macroscopic levels and the symbolic representations of chemistry (Johnstone, 1993; Kozma, Russell, Jones, Marx, & Davis, 1996; Van Driel, Verloop, & de Vos, 1998). This difficulty deserves particular attention because it is a common problem to all science disciplines where students must coordinate different descriptions and representations of a phenomenon. We initiated *The Connected Chemistry Curriculum Project* to address these challenges through the iterative development of software tools for learning secondary chemistry and the creation of a longitudinal curriculum framework with diverse learning activities. We developed CCC from three design principles, which are abstractions that connect features of the curriculum to a rationale (Kali, 2006) grounded in empirical studies of learning in chemistry:

(1) Encourage teachers and students to make their level of perspective explicit and to connect different levels. Given evidence that students come to chemistry instruction with a bias for reasoning about molecular phenomena from macroscopic perspectives (e.g., Stieff, Yip, & Ryu, 2013), CCC employs activities that provide multiple opportunities for students to state explicitly their level of perspective (i.e., macroscopic, submicroscopic, and symbolic) through drawing and written explanation with activities.

(2) Model scientific inquiry and argumentation practices relevant to chemistry. CCC includes activities that provide students with direct visual access to virtual chemical phenomena with explicit scaffolds to support data collection and link observations to claims and warrants (Gilbert, 2005). Curriculum materials support teachers with methods to model how to make relevant and meaningful observations and reflect on student claims during group discussion.

(3) Make explicit the utility of multiple representations and models to support students in using different representations and models effectively. To be successful in chemistry, students must learn to coordinate multiple representations and models of a given phenomenon and use them appropriately to explain unseen phenomena (Kozma et al., 1996). CCC activities encourage students to explore the utility of different representations—such as diagrams, molecular models, and text—for communicating and offer explicit justifications for using a representation to make a claim.

These design principles informed the structure of the curriculum, and they are embodied in activities that include visualizations designed in Java, Flash, and

NetLogo (Wilensky, 1999). CCC activities encourage active exploration using both virtual and laboratory environments. Using the visualizations, students virtually manipulate a chemical reaction under study in the laboratory, where they make predictions about the outcome of their manipulations and compare their observations with their predictions. Consequently, students receive extensive feedback from the visualization about their developing understanding. Such active exploration with simulations combats problems with poor engagement, low retention, and lack of conceptual change in science classrooms (de Jong & Lazonder, 2014).

Overview of the Connected Chemistry Curriculum

CCC was built to include nine *conceptual units* (Modeling Matter, Solutions, Reactions, Gas Laws, Kinetics, Thermodynamics, Equilibrium, Acids & Bases, and Nuclear). Each *unit* consists of multiple *lessons* that students complete within one to three 45-minute class sessions. Lessons make use of different *activities* to promote conceptual change and representational competence. Every unit comprises three core activities—*laboratory, simulation*, and *discussion activities*. In *laboratory activities* students perform a standard laboratory experiment that guides them to explore and observe macroscopic properties of chemical phenomena. In *simulation activities* pairs of students explore a simulation to understand the nature of the submicroscopic interactions that are responsible for the macroscopic events observed in the laboratory. Each pair of students is guided to explore the simulation, make predictions, and generate explanations about the relations between the submicroscopic and macroscopic world. In *discussion activities* the teacher guides students through a synthesis of their observations to discuss the conceptual underpinnings that link submicroscopic interactions with their macroscopic observations. Full units with accompanying teacher materials are available at http://connchem.org.

Focal Design Process Elements

The development of CCC began in 2004 through collaboration between one design-based researcher and a group of five chemistry teachers. Working with two NetLogo simulations that modeled chemical equilibrium and state changes, the design team began by creating a set of activities that would help students use the simulations to support their learning in the classroom. This early collaboration would lay the foundation of the design philosophy the project would pursue over the next 10 years: materials development would always employ a "work circle" (Reiser et al., 2000) that included multiple stakeholders, not just university-employed design-based researchers, at the center of the design effort through all stages of development and assessment. The design philosophy recognizes that each stakeholder brings diverse expertise to the work circle. University researchers bring expertise in development, domain knowledge, and technology. Teachers bring expertise of effective classroom practices, local science standards, and available resources. Developers bring expertise in software affordances and constraints and design solutions. Finally, students bring expertise in the efficacy of materials, their relevance, and usability (Druin, 2005). Work circles have been successful in the development and sustained use of technology-based activities for teaching science elsewhere (Brown & Edelson, 1998; Penuel, Fishman, Cheng, & Sabelli, 2011; Reiser et al., 2000), and the CCC Project team strongly advocates for their use in the design of learning environments. In particular, work circles are well suited for developing learning environments that can complement existing curricular materials such that they integrate with local classroom norms and practices rather than obviate them (Heckman & Peterman, 1996).

Previous studies on computer-based curricula indicate that visualization tools hold potential learning benefits for students, but they can be a significant source of confusion when in the classroom. For example, students do not always engage in appropriate scientific explorations using visualization tools without substantial support from instructors or curriculum materials (de Jong & van Joolingen, 1998; Lowe, 1999). Moreover, the rich interfaces and multiple opportunities for exploration that computers provide can distract students from the intended learning goals without careful planning (Kozma & Russell, 1997). The CCC work circle attempted to overcome these challenges with iterative cycles of design, enactment, and research where one cycle informed the next. We assert that the most effective design process includes input from multiple stakeholders who are working across multiple school contexts: by acknowledging the resources and constraints of teachers and students from diverse settings, curriculum designers can better develop materials that are more responsive to the needs of different users.

We accomplish this with a seven-step process model pursued by three subgroups of the work circle: the *development team*, the *evaluation team*, and the *teacher implementers*. Briefly, each curriculum activity is developed by the work circle as follows (Figure 8.1). In Step I the development team drafts materials according to the principles outlined earlier. In Step II these materials are reviewed by the evaluation team to determine whether they meet stated principles, their degree of alignment with content standards, and their attention to local constraints. In Step III the development team revises the drafted materials based on recommendations from Step II. In Step IV the teacher implementers pilot the activity in their classrooms. During an enactment, members of the work circle make field observations of instruction and conduct formative and summative assessments of student learning. In Step V the development team revises curriculum materials to attend to issues documented in Step IV. In Step VI the evaluation team again reviews the materials. Finally, in Step VII the development team again revises curriculum materials to attend to recommendations from Step VI. These seven steps comprise one iteration of the design cycle employed to produce a set of

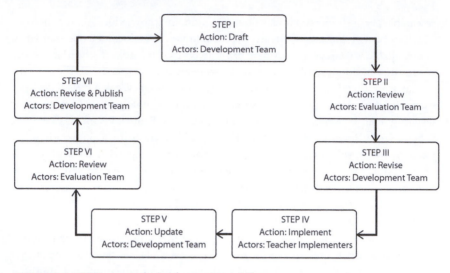

FIGURE 8.1 CCC materials development workflow

materials that are then released to the user community. As the curriculum project continues, we employ this process model annually to revise existing materials as we learn about the affordances of CCC for supporting the teaching and learning of chemistry.

Design Story: Challenges and Opportunities Designing the Connected Chemistry Curriculum

The design process we employ today on the project took many years to develop. At the start of our work, we looked to the research literature for guidelines on how to initiate a project on designing a technology-infused curriculum but found little guidance. Instead, we found a wealth of theoretical models that aimed to demonstrate the design process (e.g., Collins, Joseph, & Bielaczyc, 2004; Joseph, 2004) or outline goals for designing learning environments (e.g., diSessa & Cobb, 2004). The vast majority of work in the learning sciences seemed only to describe the end products of design work or to describe learning processes that a novel design supported. We found no clear guidance from the design research literature on how to create an effective work circle or how design teams tackled issues that arose along the way. Rather, this knowledge seemed to be distributed across the design community, and we found ourselves frequently turning to e-mail and phone calls for help.

Although members of the design community were forthcoming with advice, we endured a lengthy cycle of trial-and-error attempts to tweak our design process so that it worked to meet the needs of students and teachers as well as our research goals. On this journey we encountered three significant challenges that shaped the design process we use today. First, we experienced challenges creating and sustaining work circles in each location where development activities would take place. Second, we found ourselves frequently navigating trade-offs between constraints on our resources and our design aspirations. Third, we struggled to employ a design process in live classrooms during the school year. Although we perceived these challenges as setbacks at the time, we are mindful that they were also major learning experiences that allowed us to improve our design process and our workflow. We elaborate on each challenge and our attempts to resolve them over the project history.

Establishing, Sustaining, and Expanding a Design Work Circle

To build a curriculum that meets the needs of multiple stakeholders, the CCC Project advocates for including students and teachers in the design process together with disciplinary experts, developers, and design-based researchers. Early in the design history of the curriculum, the representation of each stakeholder was limited: the first work circle members included only one design-based researcher and a group of volunteer teachers. Teachers, researchers, and students are busy with full-time commitments, and their experiences with universities and researchers tend to be one-time events. From the early years of the project, we struggled to find work circle members who represented all stakeholders as we relied mainly on word-of-mouth referrals. Those who did join the project were often transient, and we were challenged to sustain participation for a few months let alone an entire school year.

At the time, we were deeply frustrated by this challenge, but in retrospect our expectations of members and the incentives we had offered clearly precipitated this challenge. In our rush to innovate, we placed significant demands on all work circle members with the expectation of a long-term commitment and sustained effort on the design team. Moreover, to partner effectively, we expected members to work collaboratively, to share their ideas freely, and to volunteer their time. With no training in group management, we were hard pressed to reach these goals, and we found early on that our approach to recruiting members yielded poor results. Similarly, the norms that we set in the work circle did not facilitate the collaborative interaction we desired among members who did commit to long-term participation.

To address this challenge, we developed three strategies that addressed issues with work circle recruitment, incentive structures, and group interactions. First, to address issues of recruitment we abandoned our reliance on referrals and moved to cast a wide net to find members at a variety of institutions in our local area. We developed an application and interview process to identify teachers and students who expressed a strong commitment to improving student learning through curriculum development, displayed a willingness to collaborate with others in a group, and were receptive to feedback on their work products.

Actionably, to find the best people to populate the work circles, we put out job announcements and conducted formal interviews and obtained references for all work circle roles, whether they were teachers, students, developers, or researchers. For each nonstudent applicant, we sought input from coworkers and supervisors about the applicant's time management skills, productivity, self-motivation, and collegiality. We also sought examples of prior work that demonstrated the applicant's relevant skill set.

Second, we addressed issues with sustaining participation by instituting incentive structures to compensate work circle members for their time and effort. Our early naiveté and our lack of external funding at the time led us to rely on group members who would donate time out of a willingness to improve student experiences in school. Although each member always expressed such willingness, practical constraints made it challenging for them to sustain their initial effort. Our simple solution was to compensate all work circle members for their participation. Although this seemed a straightforward solution, constraints on grant expenditures and human resources policies complicated matters significantly; university students had pay limits, teachers could not be paid for effort expended during school hours, and faculty pay had to be deferred to summer months. Although initially declaring that paying work circle members for their time was not possible, business personnel at each respective institution were able to surmount these challenges with creative (and legal!) approaches.

Third, to address challenges around group interactions, we employed strategies from business to improve our work process and establish a true community of practice (Wenger, 2000). Through the early years of the project, we found the work circles, once established, would quickly devolve into traditional hierarchies where students deferred to teachers, teachers deferred to project researchers, and everyone deferred to university faculty members who joined the team. This hierarchy was in stark violation of our design philosophy, and no matter how strongly we advocated for equal participation among all members, it remained elusive. To address this we reached out to colleagues working in the business sector to learn about effective project management strategies proven to work in industry. This discussion led one intrepid graduate student researcher in the group, Meg Garvin, to employ *faultline theory* (Lau & Murnighan, 2005) to help us modify our group processes. Faultline theory asserts that there are hidden social relationships (i.e., faultlines) between individuals and groups in a team that can create fractures that interrupt group productivity. To break down the structural hierarchies that were being re-created in the work circle, we made a concerted effort to encourage group dialogues where each member could voice his or her expectations of the group and assumptions about the motivations of other group members. We also distributed diverse tasks (i.e., high value, low value, complex, and simple) across group members so that all members could experience multiple roles, regardless of their status outside the work circle. For example, the project principal investigator (PI) was sometimes engaged with formatting curriculum workbooks (a simple, low-value task), and students some-times made executive decisions about design elements (a complex, high-value task). We also worked to help student and teacher work circle members—who often expressed less confidence in the work circle—to see that their effort was valued and equivalent to that of researchers or university faculty working on the team. To do this, we held meetings to review developed materials not only at the university, but also at partner schools, cafes, and district offices. In these meetings, we worked to make clear how recommendations and input from each member led to a specific curriculum modification. We also worked to ensure that all print materials produced by the group acknowledged the specific mem-bers who contributed to their development, and in cases where participants were required to remain anonymous for confidentiality, we held private meetings to acknowledge their contributions.

Our work circle structure evolved over time, but new designers can learn from our experience. By building in processes that break down structural hierar-chies from the start of the project, designers can better spend time and resources elsewhere. This also increases the effectiveness of group communication. By dividing work tasks among work circle members no matter their roles on the project, the entire team can better adopt a shared goal with clear expectations. Finally, new designers can build in design-sharing moments where all stakehold-ers see their value on a team. This is especially important for volunteers!

Mediating Conflicts Between Design Aspirations and Available Resources

The strategies we employed to improve our group process were effective at building a work circle with shared commitments, accountability, and effort that came online fully in the fourth year of the project and continues today. Although resolving group process issues was necessary to build CCC effectively, other challenges loomed. As described earlier, the CCC work circle was instantiated to leverage the diverse expertise of its members to address a well-documented obstacle facing chemistry learners and teachers. To do this, the group aspired to develop a curriculum that sharply diverged from traditional instructional prac-tices where teachers dictate notes to students. Although seemingly innocuous, our aspiration presented a significant challenge as we came to realize that our design decisions often exceeded the resources, both material and human, we had available to realize them.

This challenge and our strategies for overcoming it are best exemplified with one design decision that was made by the work circle in the fifth year of the project. Building on the extensive literature on representational competence, we aimed to create a curriculum that used consistent representational systems in a virtual environment with high physical fidelity that students could manipulate so that they could deduce general laws about chemical properties. This decision required us to (1) create a novel representational system to help students distinguish chemical species; (2) build a virtual environment using these representations that had high cognitive fidelity to support learning *and* high physical fidelity (Collins, 1996) so that students could interact with it as if they were manipulating real chemical systems; and (3) create activities that would help students achieve CCC learning objectives that were consistent with local district standards. These goals would greatly tax the resources of the work circle and often put us in direct conflict with the expectations of stakeholders outside of the work circle.

The primary constraint we faced was human. Our goals required a massive effort by all the work circle members. The designers, teachers, and students were tasked with inventing a representational system that contained features that were familiar to veteran teachers, but easily apprehended by novice students. Accomplishing this required extensive storyboarding by designers, revision by teachers, and usability testing by students over a 5-month period. Figure 8.2 illustrates three alternative designs for our representation of ions that the team debated for several months. Concurrently, our developers were tasked to work with our content experts to use this representational system to create a microworld in Java that simulated all known chemical and physical laws.

Although we were fortunate enough to have funding from the U.S. Department of Education that allowed us to employ two content experts, three designers, five teachers, four students, and two developers, this was not sufficient for us to accomplish our goals with a reasonable workload. Group members

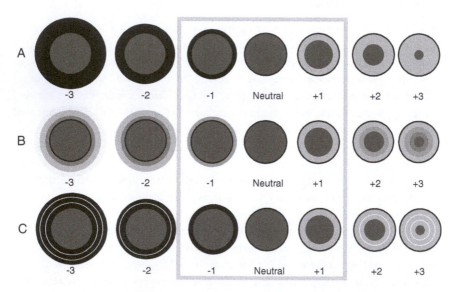

FIGURE 8.2 Alternative designs considered for ions in the CCC representational system

were frequently working 70-hour weeks into the early morning hours to create materials that would be deployed for testing that day. In some cases, this workload resulted from the aspirations of our work circle to create a novel microworld and component curriculum materials in a short time frame. In other cases, we were encumbered by our own skills. For example, working in an academic setting with fixed resources, we were not always able to hire experienced developers who demanded industry salaries. Often, we could only afford to hire less experienced developers (or sometimes graduate students). These team members worked tirelessly to train on the job to acquire the skills necessary to realize our design decisions. Although we often sought ways to lighten the workload, we were never as successful as we hoped to be: a budget in excess of $1.75 million over a 5-year period was sufficient to employ only half of the personnel needed.

Our biggest takeaway from this process that can help new designers is to budget competitive salaries if you are developing software. In hindsight, we should have allocated more funding to hire developers because the crux of our curriculum was new software. This would have ensured an end product that was developed by an expert, reduced "learning on the job" requirements, increased productivity, and boosted team morale. Those extra work hours that were spent on these tasks could have then been reallocated to other staff and tasks.

Designing in Real Time in Real School Contexts

Our design philosophy led us to work together with multiple stakeholders who represented different groups of students in schools with access to different resources (e.g., charter, magnet, urban, selective enrollment, suburban). Moreover, we aimed to complete multiple iterations of our design cycle to improve our materials, which required us to conduct our development and revision activities during the school year to maximize feedback from our stakeholders on materials as they were produced. Although these decisions ultimately led us to develop a complete curriculum that was significantly improved with each revision, they presented unique challenges to our team that exacerbated our workload and complicated our research activity.

By choosing to develop materials in real time, we implemented a production timeline to ensure that all materials were ready for classroom use according to our teacher implementers' curriculum schedule. Because of our desire to work with multiple stakeholders, we encountered challenges with different academic calendars. For example, our partner suburban schools started up to 3 weeks earlier than the urban schools. We were equally challenged to support teachers who paced their classrooms differently; teachers varied not only on the dates they began a unit, but also on the length of time they would spend on that unit. This resulted in a timeline that often involved curriculum activities undergoing revision while concurrently studying other activities in the field.

Meeting the real deadline of an academic calendar and the different needs of teachers was an arduous task, and we employed simple project management strategies to address it. Again, we had to look to colleagues in business and friends working in industry for guidance as we found ourselves well versed in design theory and design experiments but limited in project management training. First, we employed Gantt charts to manage the development and revision of each unit on its own timeline to stage the design process incrementally toward a deadline that was set as the first day of implementation in a partner school. Second, we implemented clear policies on division of labor and accountability for all team members. This resulted in an assembly line structure where one team member would hand off partially completed activities to another team member who would add more components. This process allowed us to identify bottlenecks in production and address them quickly to stay on schedule. Our process was not infallible, and flexibility was again key, as unexpected schedule changes from teachers and schools often required us to update our timelines dynamically.

Because our project aimed to study science learning in the context of our design work, we also were tasked with collecting large amounts of data on how students and teachers experienced the curriculum as it was developed. To do this we videotaped nearly every day that a curriculum activity was in use and enlisted teachers to tape themselves with small digital cameras to distribute the effort when work circle researchers were scheduled to be in two places at once. We administered an achievement assessment after each unit was completed and also interviewed several participating students after they completed a unit. This work was ongoing annually as we aimed to identify the impact of curriculum revisions on learning processes and outcomes. In a perfectly controlled laboratory, such data collection activities are demanding, but uncomplicated.

Real school settings, however, have static calendars that are frequently interrupted, and this greatly complicated our work. We contended with unplanned pep rallies, fire drills, snow days, special schedules for school events, field trips, teacher sick days or personal leaves, student sick days, student attrition, testing, and resource allotment that disrupted data collection. To address issues that arose from a school setting not being a controlled laboratory, we worked closely with partner teachers and school administrators so that we were in constant communication from day one about the implementation plans. When a teacher showed interest in participating, we met with school leadership so that they were involved in the decision to use CCC materials in the school. This helped ensure that administrators were aware of the unique challenges and benefits that a CCC-participating teacher would face during the school year and could work with us to accommodate schedule changes. We also added "buffer zones" to the implementation of each unit to ensure that schedule disruptions would not prevent students from receiving adequate time with CCC materials before they completed an achievement assessment.

Our efforts to include administrators in our implementation plan also helped facilitate daily access to schools. Early in our work, researchers would often be delayed by setup time, regular security checks upon entry, or, in some cases, random security checks when a guard mistook a younger team member for a truant student wandering the halls. To address these issues, we designed polo shirts embroidered with the CCC logo for team members to wear when visiting schools. These shirts allowed employees to easily identify us and reduced many of the complications that third-party researchers face. Some administrators also helped us secure employee badges that we could show at the front desk for easy entry and access to storage areas where we could store data collection materials to streamline setup. Including school leadership in our process mitigated many of the common challenges education researchers face and yielded additional benefits: our participating teachers reported they were more confident in implementing new methods with administrator support, and our dissemination efforts were facilitated by administrator networks.

Because this aspect of the process was so important to our study, it was one of our biggest areas of personal development as researchers-turned-project managers. The success of any project hinges on a realistic timeline with clear roles and expectations for each person at each stage. New designers will set themselves up for a more successful project by having a realistic calendar in advance of the project with flexible time built in as a buffer zone. It is also important to anticipate various obstacles that could impede data collection and plan for them. We often research the various ways in which students understand concepts, and we should apply that same logic to our research projects. What are the various ways in which we might encounter issues? How can we build a "Plan B" into our design as a back-up plan? In our case, we provided each teacher with a camera and purchased uniforms for our staff to save time. These are lessons that were learned over time, but we will certainly implement them again in the future.

Discussion

These challenges represent only a sample of the diversity of obstacles that we faced on the project with respect to design. We were successful at overcoming some challenges, such as group process; however, we were not always able to fully eliminate every challenge, such as workload. Specific challenges require targeted strategies to address them, but we have found that collaborating with team members who are both creative and flexible is the most important factor for achieving ambitious design goals. It was the creativity and flexibility of our partner teachers, students, and researchers that allowed us ultimately to produce a set of curriculum materials that today are readily used by teachers and students across the globe. Of course, no curriculum is a static product, and we continue our work today to revise CCC materials as our understanding of learning and teaching is improved by our own research and the work of others in the learning sciences, science education, and chemistry education communities.

As we continue this work, we strive to improve not only our materials, but also our design process. When we began building CCC, we had little guidance from design-based research literature on how to go about our work. Design-based researchers expend significant effort studying the impact of their designs on learners, but we see too little discussion of the pragmatic aspects of design work among members of the community. This chapter presents a significant advancement of the discussion, but considerable work remains outstanding to demonstrate the relative efficacy of alternative design process models for developing educational innovations. It is our hope that by relating part of our design history here, we have offered some useful advice to new generations of design-based researchers that will help them to anticipate pitfalls and opportunities as they begin work on their own innovations.

Acknowledgments

The authors would like to thank all of the teachers and students who helped in the development of CCC materials over the course of the project. The efforts reported here were supported at various times by grants from the Maryland Higher Education Commission (ITQ09708, ITQ10814) and the U.S. Department of Education Institute for Education Science (R305A100992). The opinions expressed are those of the authors and do not represent the views of these agencies.

References

Brown, M., & Edelson, D.C. (1998). Software in context: Designing for students, teachers, and classroom enactment. In A.S. Bruckman, M. Guzdial, J. Kolodner, & A. Ram (Eds.), *Proceedings of the third international conference of the learning sciences* (pp. 63–69). Charlottesville, VA: AACE.

Collins, A. (1996). Design issues for learning environments. In S. Vosniadou, R. Glaser, E. De Corte, & H. Mandl (Eds.), *International perspectives on the psychological foundations of technology-based learning environments* (pp. 347–361). Hillsdale, NJ: Erlbaum.

Collins, A., Joseph, D., & Bielaczyc, K. (2004). Design research: Theoretical and methodological issues. *Journal of the Learning Sciences, 13*(1), 15–42.

de Jong, T., & Lazonder, A.W. (2014) The guided discovery learning principle in multimedia learning. In R.E. Mayer (Ed.), *The Cambridge handbook of multimedia learning* (2nd ed., pp. 371–390). Cambridge: Cambridge university press.

de Jong, T., & van Joolingen, W.R. (1998). Scientific discovery learning with computer simulations of conceptual domains. *Review of Educational Research, 68*(2), 179–201.

diSessa, A.A., & Cobb, P. (2004). Ontological innovation and the role of theory in design experiments. *Journal of the Learning Sciences, 13*(1), 77–103.

Druin, A. (2005). What children can teach us: Developing digital libraries for children with children. *Library Quarterly, 75*(1), 20–41.

Gilbert, J. K. (2005). Visualization: A metacognitive skill in science and science education. In J. K. Gilbert (Ed.), *Visualization in science education* (pp. 9-27). Dordrecht, The Netherlands: Springer.

Heckman, P., & Peterman, F. (1996). Indigenous invention: New promises for school reform. *Teachers College Record, 98*(2), 307–327.

Johnstone, A.H. (1993). The development of chemistry teaching. *Journal of Chemical Education, 70*(9), 701–705.

Joseph, D. (2004). The practice of design-based research: Uncovering the interplay between design, research, and the real-world context. *Educational Psychology, 39*(4), 235–242.

Kali, Y. (2006). Collaborative knowledge building using the design principles database. *International Journal of Computer-Supported Collaborative Learning, 1*(2), 187–201.

Kozma, R., & Russell, J. (1997). Multimedia and understanding: Expert and novice responses to different representations of chemical phenomena. *Journal of Research in Science Teaching, 34*(9), 949–968.

Kozma, R., Russell, J., Jones, T., Marx, N., & Davis, J. (1996). The use of multiple, linked representations to facilitate science understanding. In S. Vosniadou, R. Glaser, E. De Corte, & H. Mandl (Eds.), *International perspectives on the psychological foundations of technology-based learning environments* (pp. 41–60). Hillsdale, NJ: Erlbaum.

Lau, D.C., & Murnighan, J.K. (2005). Interactions within groups and subgroups: The effects of demographic faultlines. *Academy of Management Journal, 48*(4), 645–659.

Levy, S., & Wilensky, U. (2009a). Crossing levels and representations: The Connected Chemistry (CC1) curriculum. *Journal of Science Education and Technology, 18*(3), 224–242.

Levy, S., & Wilensky, U. (2009b). Students' learning with the Connected Chemistry (CC1) curriculum: Navigating the complexities of the particulate world. *Journal of Science Education and Technology, 18*(3), 243–254.

Lowe, R.K. (1999). Extracting information from an animation during complex visual learning. *European Journal of Psychology of Education, 14*(2), 225–244.

Penuel, W., Fishman, B., Cheng, B., & Sabelli, N. (2011). Organizing research and development at the intersection of learning, implementation, and design. *Educational Researcher, 40*(7), 3331–3337.

Reiser, B.J., Spillane, J.P., Steinmuller, F., Sorsa, D., Carney, K., & Kyza, E. (2000). Investigating the mutual adaptation process in teachers' design of technology-infused curricula. In B. Fishman & S. O'Connor-Divelbiss (Eds.), *Proceedings of the fourth international conference of the learning sciences* (pp. 342–349). Mahwah, NJ: Erlbaum.

Ryan, S., Yip, J., Stieff, M., & Druin, A. (2013). Cooperative inquiry as a community of practice. In N. Rummel, M. Kapur, M. Nathan, & S. Puntambekar (Eds.), *Proceedings of the 10th international conference on computer-supported collaborative learning* (pp. 145–148). Madison, WI: ISLS.

Stieff, M. (2005). Connected chemistry–A novel modeling environment for the chemistry classroom. *Journal of Chemical Education, 82*(3), 489–493.

Stieff, M. (2011a). Fostering representational competence through argumentation with multi-representational displays. *Proceedings of the 9th international conference on computer-supported collaborative learning* (Vol. 1, pp. 288–295). Mahwah, NJ: Erlbaum.

Stieff, M. (2011b). Improving representational competence using multi-representational learning environments. *Journal of Research in Science Teaching, 48*(10), 1137–1158.

Stieff, M., & McCombs, M. (2006). Increasing representational fluency with visualization tools. *Proceedings of the seventh International Conference of the Learning Sciences (ICLS)* (Vol. 1, pp. 730–736). Mahwah, NJ: Erlbaum.

Stieff, M., Nighelli, T., Yip, J., Ryan, S., & Berry, A. (2012). *The connected chemistry curriculum* (Vols. 1–9). Chicago, IL: University of Illinois.

Stieff, M., Yip, J., & Ryu, M. (2013). Speaking across levels—teacher and student discourse practices in the chemistry classroom. *Chemistry Education Research & Practice, 14*(4), 376–389.

Stieff, M., & Wilensky, U. (2003). Connected chemistry—Incorporating interactive simulations into the chemistry classroom. *Journal of Science Education & Technology, 12*(3), 285–302.

Van Driel, J.H., Verloop, N., & de Vos, W. (1998). Developing science teachers' pedagogical content knowledge. *Journal of Research in Science Teaching, 35*(6), 673–695.

Wenger, E. (2000). *Communities of practice: Learning, meaning, and identity.* Cambridge, UK: Cambridge University Press.

Wilensky, U. (1999). *NetLogo* (Version 3.0) [Computer Program]. Evanston, IL: Center for Connected Learning and Computer Based Modeling, Northwestern University. Retrieved August 3, 2015 from http://ccl.northwestern.edu/netlogo.

9

MAKING IT REAL

Transforming a University and Museum Research Collaboration Into a Design Product

Palmyre Pierroux and Rolf Steier

Introduction

In design scholarship there are few overlaps between studies of *design as a discipline* and the practice of *design-based research* (Barab, 2006; Hoadley, 2004). The former, according to Cross (2007), "means design studied on its own terms, within its own rigorous culture, based on a reflective practice of designing" (p. 3). The aim of design-based research, on the other hand, is to advance the quality of learning theories and learning resources by designing and studying interventions in naturalistic educational settings. Therefore, as noted in the introduction of this book, the *designing* that goes into design-based research (DBR) experiments, interventions, and pilot studies does not often receive the same critical reflection as do changes in learning processes and institutional practices. There are many explanations for this. First, prototypes with a mid-level range of technology readiness are often sufficient to generate data for design-based research and its focus on iteratively developing theoretical constructs of learning. In other words, the level of refinement required for commercial implementation is not typically part of the iterative design processes in DBR. As Hoadley (2004) explains, the methodological goal of DBR is to move beyond documenting the success or failure of a particular design or intervention, to study social interactions, personal experiences, and institutional aspects of the designed intervention as a holistic unit of analysis. Second, learning researchers, external partners, and information scientists bring different roles, practices, and areas of expertise to collaboration in design-based research projects, making a shared framing of "design" work difficult to achieve across multiple professions (Jornet & Jahreie, 2011; Jornet & Steier, 2015). As DBR increasingly involves institutional partners (teachers, museum educators, and other professionals) in the co-design of interventions, research may focus more on understanding how tensions between different partners' values and skills emerge and are resolved than on how these are linked to changes in the actual object of design (Haapasaari & Kerosuo, 2015; Jahreie & Krange, 2011; Macdonald, 2002). In short, the object of design is framed by different kinds of activity, with outcomes that are not often viewed in relation to one another.

In this chapter, we present the story of VisiTracker, a prototype created for a design-based research project, and its development into a product and service for use in the commercial marketplace. We follow the entire design trajectory to understand how transformations in the design object affected the different roles and perspectives of the multiprofessional participants and institutions involved in the process. Based on project documents, interviews, and meeting notes collected over a nearly 3-year period, we address two research questions related to the design studies field: What are some key differences in design approaches for research and commercial contexts, respectively? How do perspectives on value creation vary and change among different partners in a multiprofessional collaboration when the object and outcome of a design-based research activity is transformed into a research-based designing activity?

Focal Design Process Elements

This chapter focuses on the ways in which elements of a design process change over time for different partners involved in the activity of taking a prototype from a research project and developing it as a commercial project. The analytical approach is framed by perspectives in cultural historical activity theory (CHAT) to distinguish between the institutional settings of university, museum, and university lab as "activity systems with different historical objects, functions, and norms and directions for their work" (Jahreie & Krange, 2011, p. 177). An important point in CHAT is that the object of activity is constantly evolving and changing, and multiprofessional teams must thus negotiate different object orientations to succeed in their collaborative work (Engeström, 1987). Accordingly, we understand the development of VisiTracker as an evolving object of activity, mediated by different types of design processes (i.e., ideation, specifications, testing, documentation, prioritizing iterations) in the multiprofessional team of researchers, curators, and interaction designers. As the object of design activity changed, the outcomes were also transformed in terms of partners' different perceptions of value creation, that is, the "what" and "how" of values they wished to create (Dorst, 2011).

Specifically, we describe design process elements in the development of VisiTracker, which is a tablet-based research tool (Figure 9.1) and online portal initially conceived and developed for museum curators and educators to conduct and analyze real-time observations of individual and group behaviors of visitors, mapped to locations and displays in exhibitions (Pierroux, Qvale, Steier, & Sauge, 2014). However, as an observational tool, it also has the potential to be

FIGURE 9.1   Screenshot of VisiTracker Interface

adapted for use in other contexts and public spaces, from urban design to studies of shopping behaviors. VisiTracker allows individual and coordinated groups of trained "observers" to communicate; note visitor types; track groups' movements; tag behaviors with customizable interaction categories updated on the fly; and link observations with video and audio recordings, interviews, surveys, and other data types. In the portal, the users access analyses of these rich datasets in the form of customizable visualizations (e.g., cluster analysis, dwell time, attraction rate, and frequencies of groups' actions). The portal also allows users to organize studies and manage recorded data as part of a comprehensive system displaying demographics, filtering and combining datasets, and comparing aggregated user data over time.

Observations of this type are particularly useful for exhibition designers and museums in formative and summative evaluation phases of new exhibitions. From an exhibition designer's perspective, visitor studies are useful in testing different features of a design at different phases of development. Museums use such knowledge to evaluate the success of new exhibitions by understanding more general patterns of behavior as well as how specific displays engage visitors. Technically and conceptually, VisiTracker is an innovation in tablet-based applications currently available on international markets in terms of the unique combination of real-time features that allow observers to note individual and small-group interactions at a high level of granularity.

The design of VisiTracker involved collaboration among learning researchers at a university; a senior developer, software engineer, interaction designer, and the director at a lab at the same university; educators, curators, and special advisors at a national art museum; and innovation consultants from the university specializing in the commercialization of research that may "benefit society and contribute to value creation" (retrieved from http://www.inven2.com). We use the VisiTracker story to reflect on how design thinking was made "real" for the different partners during the collaboration as the object of design activity moved from a research context to a commercialization project that is currently ongoing. According to Dorst (2011), design thinking involves specific abilities and deliberate ways of reasoning in design practice, the core concepts of which may be understood in terms of formal logic. However, as general interest in design thinking has emerged as a new paradigm for problem solving in a broad range of professions, multiple theories and models have been proposed, and the term is used more to describe a general orientation than a specific set of procedures or reasoning pattern. In this chapter, we use the term design thinking in the sense proposed by Dorst (2011), reflecting on elements of design reasoning in different conditions and framings of *value creation*. The following VisiTracker design story traces transformations in design thinking as the object of activity became oriented toward a different kind of outcome, one with societal and practical value beyond its relevance for the initial research project.

Design Story: VisiTracker

VisiTracker emerged as a kind of secondary outcome from a nationally financed research project, which had the larger aim of investigating how digital and social media affect interpretive practices in museums and cultural heritage organizations. Design-based research (Barab, 2006; Hoadley, 2004) was the main approach used in the project, entailing a series of interventions in existing educational and curatorial practices in the partner institution, a national art museum. Studies were conducted to analyze the cognitive, communicative, and social challenges that new types of activities and digital tools posed for visitors and curators alike, with the aim of advancing the quality of digitally mediated learning in gallery spaces (Pierroux & Ludvigsen, 2013).

An important premise for the project was that the design-based research would be grounded in a process of collaboratively identifying and formulating "existing problems in practice" related to learning and digital media in the museum. Engeström (2011) calls such research approaches formative interventions, in that the institution partner articulates the starting point or initial needs that the intervention will address. This premise acknowledges that "research-driven agendas" may produce conflicts between designs directed toward research interests and designs that address the authentic concerns of stakeholders. Balancing researchers' and partners' interests in design-based research collaborations is arguably a key to effecting sustainable new practices and technologies in learning settings and gauging their societal value (Jewitt, 2006; Pierroux, 2009). In practical terms, as with principles of co-design and participatory design traditions, formative interventions are intentionally introduced processes and tools that aim to produce (jointly) constructed articulations of existing problems in practice and the design of new practices for future outcomes that may be investigated empirically (e.g., in the form of conjectures as described by Engeström (2011) and Sandoval (2013)).

In the case of VisiTracker, the idea for the tool emerged from a study of visitors in a gallery room dedicated to Edvard Munch's art in the national museum. The museum curator of education was planning to conduct informal observations of this gallery, with the aim of studying whether visitors read new texts he had recently introduced into the space. This was communicated to the researchers early on in the collaboration, and over the course of several meetings, university and museum interests became aligned in expanding this activity. We developed a paper-based instrument that mediated the study of how visitors moved and used the physical gallery space, how they interacted with each other, and how much time they spent reading labels and texts and looking at works of art. Findings from these studies were to be used by the museum to gain insight into existing labeling practices and visitor behaviors, but also by the research team for the design of new digital resources and gallery interactives that would be studied as part of the larger project.

The researchers developed the first version of the protocol based on the most widespread and established observation method in visitor studies, which entails tracking and timing visitors' movements through museums, zoos, or science centers (Yalowitz & Bronnenkant, 2009). The protocols were tested by both partners on site and then refined for actual use (Figure 9.2). The observations were scheduled and carried out in collaboration with museum staff over a 3-week period on different days and times. One instrument was used to note observations of demographic information, group size, and the amount of time spent in the gallery room. A second protocol was used to record visitors' movements on a floor plan of the gallery, mapping individual and group movements around the room, noting where they stopped and dwell time and interactions with different works of art, resources, and devices they brought into the galleries. The observers, often coordinating their work in pairs, were seated on a bench in the gallery and began to track visitor groups as they entered the doorway, recording members' movements in the room until they left. Once the group had left, the observer would start with the next new group to enter. Information about the study was conveyed to the public using discreet signage.

The researchers analyzed the data, with results that surprised the museum partners and challenged long-held assumptions about visitor demographics and behaviors. One finding involved the sequence of visitor pathways in the "Munch Room," where works had been arranged in a largely chronological progression clockwise around the room. The assumption was that visitors would tend to follow this sequence, turning left upon entering the gallery. However, we found that visitors were just as likely—if not more so—to move in the opposite direction, turning right instead of left when they entered. Moreover, the study

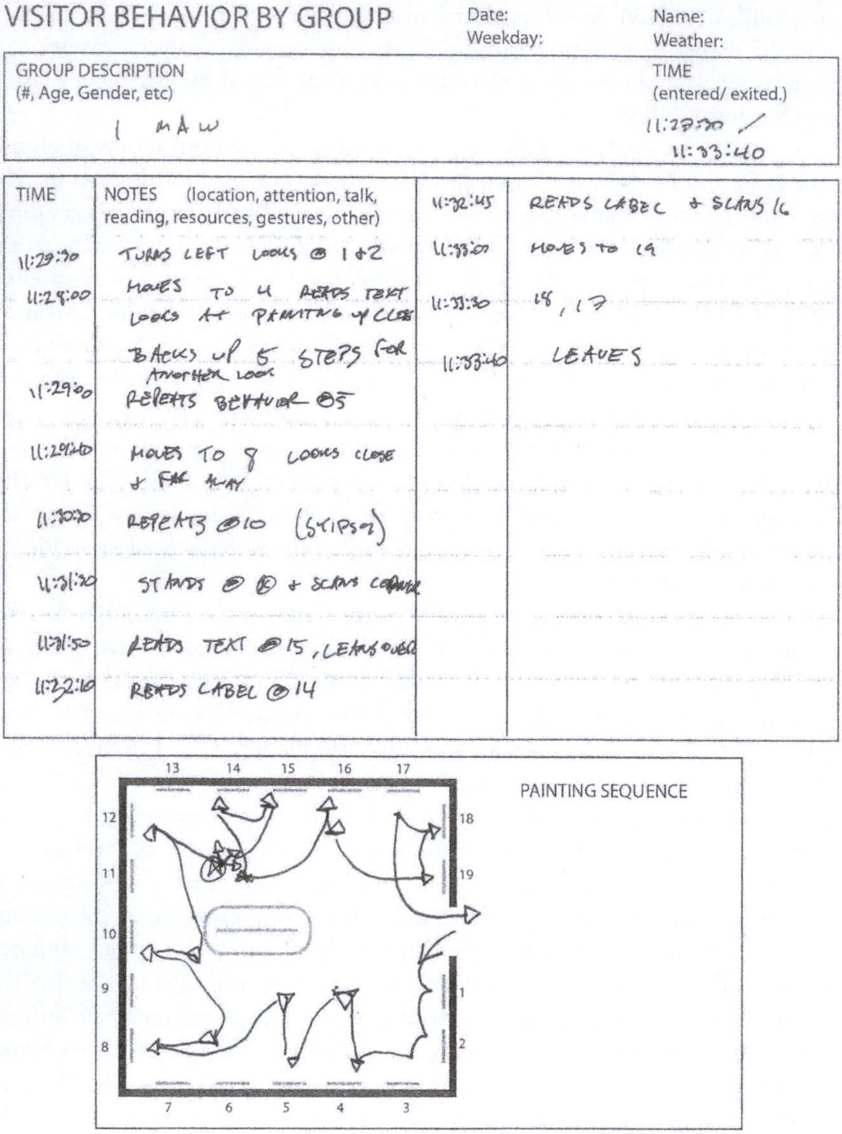

FIGURE 9.2 Paper–based observation protocols

showed that groups of two or three visitors were most common, and that visitors were much younger than the museum staff had anticipated. Importantly, the museum partners were motivated by these seemingly small findings and their implications, and they saw the potential of using such tools to expand evaluation activities in the future and to gain greater insight into visitor behaviors. At this point, through participation in an activity mediated primarily by researcher-led methods and tools, it became apparent for the museum partners that the adoption of such instruments could transform other aspects of the museum's practice.

A Digital Prototype

While conducting the observations, it became clear to one of the researchers that digitizing this tool to increase effectiveness and functionality would render it valuable for collecting data later in the project as well. It was at this point that the university lab became involved in making a simple application based on the paper protocol, financed by existing project funds allocated by the leader of the research project and additional funds from the Department of Education. Thus, the design-based research context expanded to become an activity with new partners and "design thinking" practices involving the university lab (EngageLab). The lab employs both permanent and temporary staff with backgrounds as interaction designers and software engineers in computer science (groups of four to six persons). The researchers and museum partners began meetings with designers and programmers from EngageLab to provide input regarding the scope, function, and design of VisiTracker as a digital research tool that they planned for use later in the project. The earliest iterations addressed issues regarding the touch interface, programming language, Wi-Fi connection, and data management. The first prototype was intended to be completed in time to use during the opening of the Munch project room, supplementing the primary interactional data collected by researchers using video recordings. However, due to the prioritization of other activities by both the lab and researchers, the application was not fully tested by the time of the opening and was never used for data collection in the main research project. Instead, initial testing of the application focused mainly on getting feedback on the user experience of the application and developing a survey feature that the museum wanted to use in a small visitor study.

Since the final year of the research project, the lead researcher, in consultation with the director and senior developer of the lab, secured two rounds of "innovation" funding from the Research Council of Norway and the university faculty to further develop the prototype into a market-ready product and service. This funding grounded the framing of further design activity from a commercialization perspective. In particular, the researcher's insistence on adding a web portal for analyzing, visualizing, and managing the data collected from observations was a significant move in transforming the outcome of the activity from designing a tablet-based application for use in a research project to developing a commercial product that the lab could maintain and continually improve for a potentially much broader group of users (Figure 9.3). A technology transfer office was brought on board to initiate and support a new process involving business models, marketing strategies, and inventors' rights, expanding the activity and outcomes of the multiprofessional team. These activities included

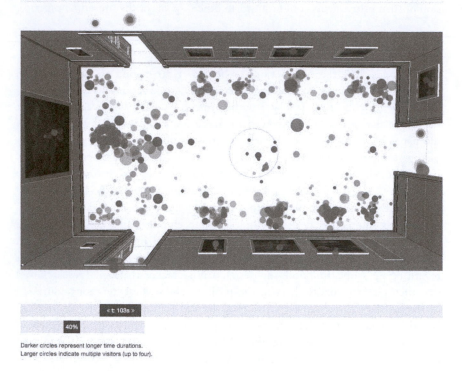

Darker circles represent longer time durations.
Larger circles indicate multiple visitors (up to four).

FIGURE 9.3 Heat map visualization in VisiTracker web portal

contract negotiations with the museum partner to secure its role as distributor of VisiTracker to a network of Norwegian museums and the securing of option contracts with potential clients outside of the museum sector. The shared aim is to establish VisiTracker in the international marketplace by early 2016.

Discussion

In this section, we zoom in on aspects of the design story to critically reflect on some key differences in approaches to designing for research and commercial contexts, respectively. We do this by examining different perspectives on *value creation* that the partners brought to the activity—university researchers, university lab, museum educators, and innovation consultants—exploring how the sociohistorical features of the respective practices were made relevant. In this way, we wish to unpack the complexities and negotiations involved in an expanding multiprofessional "problem-space" (Engeström, 1987). This will address the research question posed earlier concerning how perspectives on value creation vary and change among different partners in a multiprofessional collaboration when the object and outcome of a design-based *research* activity are transformed into a research-based *designing* activity.

Perspectives on Value Creation by University Researchers

From the perspective of the university researchers specializing in the learning sciences, the main object of the design-based research project was to study visitors' meaning making and changing practices in museums when digital interpretive resources were introduced into gallery spaces. The emergent focus on observation tools thus mediated a new design activity trajectory and outcome for both the museum and the researchers. As described later, "visitor studies" was a new practice for the museum, and in this sense, researchers were able to study this transformation in keeping with overall project aims and perspectives on value creation in research practice. The design of VisiTracker also presented opportunities to investigate methods for linking observational data with new tracking and anonymous data collection technologies.

At the same time, as the object and outcome of the VisiTracker design activity transformed and expanded toward commercialization, a set of very real tensions related to research practice also emerged. First, the participation of university researchers in commercial design activity—and writing proposals to fund it—reduces time spent on core research activity. Second, although the university emphasizes innovation and research that benefits society, design activity is not valued in the same way by leadership and peers as is the production of high-quality journal publications. From the university researchers' perspective, then, the potential to develop theoretical and methodological contributions to the learning sciences based on studies involving VisiTracker would be the primary consideration for value creation. This potential has yet to be realized, and is complicated by the fact that the methods embodied in the VisiTracker application are not geared to studies of learning, which is the core focus for the researchers.

Perspectives on Value Creation by Museum Partners

From the perspective of the museum partners, the design of VisiTracker mediated new interests, professional status, and knowledge practices in the organization. At the start of the research collaboration nearly 5 years ago, views among senior museum staff on the use of digital and social media in the museum's communication and education strategies were conflicted and underdeveloped. Moreover, the recently established education section that spanned across departments had just been dismantled by new museum leadership, which favored a curator-led, "team-based" approach within each department (architecture, art, design) to develop exhibitions and educational materials. Opportunities were thus minimized within the organization for professional identity building and knowledge sharing among staff responsible for educational and digital interpretive resources.

Importantly, aside from surveys conducted by external consultants for marketing and reporting purposes, studies of visitors were rarely conducted. The design and use of VisiTracker introduced a whole new set of activities and knowledge practices *in the museum*, in the sense of expansive transformations (Engeström, 1987). The lead participant from the museum emphasized this aspect of value creation in her presentation of the tool:

> In VisiTracker we have a flexible tool that shows us what the visitors do in our exhibitions. And when we have this knowledge, we can design, organize and plan our exhibitions better. The museum started these kinds of observations only a few years back, and we started with a simple version that has now developed into VisiTracker, which has the potential to become a very useful tool in the museum's aims to gain more knowledge about visitors' behaviors. The visualizations are available in different representations, making the findings easy to communicate among colleagues in the museum.

On the whole, the museum partners reported a general acknowledgement of the value of the kinds of skills and knowledge they have developed through the project, along with a new status associated with the practice of conceptualizing and designing digital and social media in the museum. The museum participants have reported strong interest among fellow staff members in VisiTracker and the other research-based activities in which they have participated. In addition to internal presentations and meetings, their expertise and advice on digital design has been sought in a very real sense, contributing input to digital strategies for the new museum building currently planned. The investment in time and expertise in developing VisiTracker has fostered a strong and rightful sense of ownership among the museum staff members. However, without institutional anchoring of new practices and methods at the leadership level, it is not likely that the museum will retain its currently informal role as "owner" of VisiTracker, as its main user. We are currently drafting a proposal to secure financing for maintaining and developing the tool for the museum and for providing training and support, subject to museum leadership approval. However, as "real-world" commercialization issues have become more pressing with the technological readiness of the tool, and as the activity has expanded from participation in a research project to more formal ownership of research tools and practices, it is far from certain that the value created in the museum will be sustainable, given the historical conditions for transforming institutional practices.

Perspectives on Value Creation by the University Lab

VisiTracker came at a time of transition for EngageLab. A new organizational structure at the faculty level was established for the university lab in 2013, as was a new financial plan that required transitioning into a self-funded and more independent group. A director is responsible for the staff, budget, and overall strategy. Historically, EngageLab has collaborated with researchers when it was allocated funds in research projects to conduct specific types of work. Lab members provided support to researchers in different ways, usually developing technology-based tools, applications, and prototypes for design-based research interventions and offering guidance in different modes of design thinking.

As described, the lab performed most of the technical work for VisiTracker, and its relationship to the project shifted from developing the first prototype to more recently taking ownership of the activity of commercialization. Although the researcher was mainly responsible for securing VisiTracker financing and officially functioned as project leader, she insisted that the director, senior developer, and team of engineers and interaction designers in EngageLab manage the budget, scope, and implementation of commercialization work, signaling a transfer of ownership from university researcher to university lab. A key feature of this reframing of the design activity was a change in how outcomes of *iterative processes* were understood by the multiprofessional team.

In contrast to iterative design processes directed by researchers, who were mainly concerned with tweaking prototypes and solutions to be "good enough" to implement in a study, iterations in the VisiTracker application and portal designs became more strategically prioritized based on a broader and more rigorous set of design issues (i.e., state of the art, budget, stability, user needs, testing, specifications, and documentation). Professional design management software, Liquid Planner, became the main tool used by the lab members to identify and prioritize design iterations in meetings with researchers and museum partners, mediating the multiprofessional team's work. Examples of design iterations include the implementation of "event" recordings instead of tracing pathways (Figure 9.4), an interface with toolbox overlays instead of swiping between screens, and an offline "save" mode.

Historically, collaboration in design-based research projects at the department could become fraught with tension between lab staff and researchers over decisions made regarding value creation and design outcomes. In contrast to what Dorst (2011) refers to as a more open-ended *Abduction-2* mode of design, the lab members were mostly tasked by the researchers with more conventional problem solving, dealing with issues of *what* rather than *how*, or an *Abduction-1* mode of design thinking. In the latter, the basic reasoning pattern in design thinking entails a value or outcome to create for and working principles, or rules, to achieve it. As Dorst (2011) explains, this is a form of *closed problem solving* and "often what designers and engineers do—create a design that works with a known working principle within a set scenario of value creation" (p. 524). Interviews with lab members revealed tensions between modes of design work that support a *research scenario* of value creation (i.e., developing short-lived prototypes

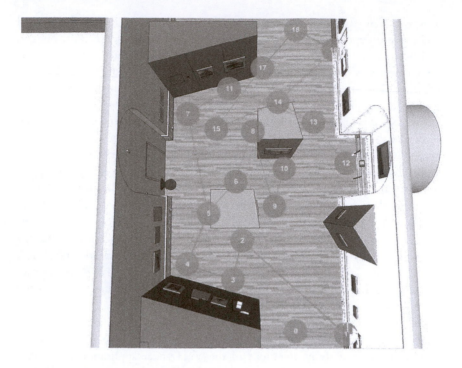

FIGURE 9.4   Group tracking visualization

that are abandoned at completion of a project) and the frequent wish of external partners (museums, schools, other organizations) to continue developing and using these products, which the lab lacked the resources to support. Moreover, as part of a community of practice, the developers, designers, and programmers see themselves as advocates for a quality of user experience that is difficult to prioritize in design-based research projects, which often have goals of generating research data as efficiently as possible. The lab director characterized this conflict between researcher and lab member views on the value of designing for quality user experience as follows:

> User experience is not necessarily a "pro" for a researcher as long as you get valid data out of it. [. . .] It's a potential conflict, since user experience is an area of expertise that may actually make the research better. So having a fruitful discussion with researchers on precisely this topic has been one of the largest challenges for the lab. To be perceived as a relevant partner means asking relevant questions in relevant situations. And then to be able to do this in a project like VisiTracker, which obviously needs a good user experience because the curators at the museum, they need to use this tool—so if they have a good user experience, they get good data.

In this sense, the lab members' perspective on value creation is linked to the opportunity to practice good design work focused on user experience and robust solutions that are tested incrementally. Moreover, the design collaboration in VisiTracker also created value for the lab in terms of a new relationship with the museum partner, and meetings and new design activities are no longer necessarily initiated and led by the researchers. There have been opportunities to provide new services involving *Abduction-2* modes of design work, which the lab views as far more interesting than the problem-solving approaches often required in design-based research collaborations. The lab now more clearly engages with its dual mandate of designing prototypes that are "robust enough" for scholarly research and developing innovative products and services with potential market and societal value. From a CHAT perspective, such change may be understood as an *expansive transformation*, a concept formulated by Engeström (1987) to describe how individuals may collectively reconceptualize the object and outcome of an activity to embrace a radically wider horizon of possibilities than in the previous mode of the activity.

At the same time, in the context of a university lab, contradictions and conflicts have emerged in the strategic and organizational transformation involved in selling products and services in the commercial marketplace and becoming self-funded. Specifically, there is a tension in that funding proposals for research and development have required a researcher to lead the work rather than lab staff. Although not a problem in the context of VisiTracker, which has the full support and interest of the researcher, there is a need for the university lab to develop expertise in securing alternative sources of capital. Overall, looking forward, a lack of expertise in developing business plans, organizing start-ups, securing venture capital, and identifying and designing for potential markets are major challenges that VisiTracker has introduced into the university lab organization. These are the realities of institutional top-down "innovation" strategies and goals, and it is perhaps important to note from a policy perspective that such inner contradictions of an activity system become "the principle of its self-movement" (Ilyenkov, 1977, p. 330). In VisiTracker, this has played out in a very concrete manner, as the multiprofessional team expanded to embrace innovation experts and market consultants, and positioned the lab director as the main translator and owner of VisiTracker's commercial success. In other words, the skills and knowledge practices that are prioritized in response to demands for autonomy and commercialization projects have real consequences for value creation and design practices in university labs, and perhaps for the university institution as well.

Conclusion

The VisiTracker story reveals how design was understood and made "real" from the respective partners' interests in design collaboration, as the participants grappled with emergent objects of activity and responded to changes in the rules, tools, and sociohistorical practices of their work. Although the multidisciplinary team established an understanding of working on the same design task, this study has shown how a network of activity systems, objects, and outcomes emerged for the different partners. The observation protocols and methods, initially developed for scholarly purposes, were quickly taken up by the museum partners, transforming existing practices by addressing a real need for in-house research. At the researchers' initiative, the paper-based instruments were designed as a tablet-based prototype for the initial research project. Subsequently, through additional funding earmarked for the commercialization of outcomes from the same research program, VisiTracker became very real for the university lab director as a vehicle for achieving institutional aims of self-funding and autonomy. This turn required collaboration between programmers from the university lab, the project researchers, the museum partner, and a consultant firm that secures intellectual property rights for the university and develops research outcomes into useful products with commercial value. Equally important for the designers and programmers in the lab was the opportunity VisiTracker afforded to establish relationships with external partners based on alternative modes of design thinking (Dorst, 2011). In sum, the "real" value discerned from this design story lies not in how an innovative tool was developed for the market from a research project, but rather in the insight it has afforded into how institutional practices may be transformed through multiprofessional design collaboration.

Acknowledgments

This research was conducted in the *Observe* project, financed by the VERDIKT program at the Research Council of Norway (2013–2014) and the Faculty of Educational Sciences, University of Oslo. We gratefully acknowledge the design and management contributions of *EngageLab* director Lars Lomell, senior developer Jeremy Toussaint, senior engineer Richard Nesnass, and interaction designers Edith Isdal and Idunn Sem at the Faculty of Educational Sciences, University of Oslo. We especially thank our collaborative partner, The National Museum of Art, Architecture and Design, and the expert contributions of Senior Advisor Anne Qvale and Senior Curator of Education Frithjof Bringager.

References

Barab, S. (2006) Design-based research: A methodological toolkit for engineering change. In K. Sawyer (Ed.), *The Cambridge handbook of the learning sciences* (pp. 151–170). Cambridge, UK: Cambridge University Press.

Cross, N. (2007). Forty years of design research. *Design Studies, 28*(1), 1–4.

Dorst, K. (2011). The core of 'design thinking' and its application. *Design Studies, 32*(6), 521–532.

Engeström, Y. (1987). *Learning by expanding: An activity-theoretical approach to developmental research.* Helsinki: Orienta-Konsultit.

Engeström, Y. (2011). From design experiments to formative interventions. *Theory & Psychology, 21*(5), 598–628.

Haapasaari, A., & Kerosuo, H. (2015). Transformative agency: The challenges of sustainability in a long chain of double stimulation. *Learning, Culture and Social Interaction, 4*(1), 37–47.

Hoadley, C.M. (2004). Methodological alignment in design-based research. *Educational Psychologist, 39*(4), 203–212. doi:10.1207/s15326985ep3904_2.

Ilyenkov, E. (1977). *Problems of dialectical materialism.* Translated by A. Bluden. Moscow: Progress Publishers.

Jahreie, C., & Krange, I. (2011). Learning in science education across school and science museums—design and development work in a multi-professional group. *Nordic Journal of Digital Literacy, 6 ER*(03), 174–188.

Jewitt, C. (2006). *Technology, literacy and learning. A multimodal approach.* London: Routledge.

Jornet, A., & Jahreie, C.F. (2011). *Designing for immersive learning environments across schools and science museums. Multi-professional conceptualizations of space.* Paper presented at the Researching Learning in Immersive Virtual Environments (ReLive 2011), Milton Keynes, UK.

Jornet, A., & Steier, R. (2015). The matter of space: Joint bodily engagement and the emergence of boundary objects during multidisciplinary design work. *Mind, Culture & Activity, 22*(2), 129–151.

Macdonald, S. (2002). *Behind the scenes at the science museum.* Oxford: Berg.

Pierroux, P. (2009). Newbies and design research: Approaches to designing a learning environment using mobile and social technologies. In G. Vavoula, A. Kukulska-Hulme, & N. Pachler (Eds.), *Researching mobile learning: Frameworks, methods and research designs* (pp. 289–316). Bern: Peter Lang.

Pierroux, P., & Ludvigsen, S. (2013). Communication interrupted: Textual practices and digital interactives in art museums. In K. Schrøder & K. Drotner (Eds.), *The connected museum: Social media and museum communication* (pp. 153–176). London: Routledge.

Pierroux, P., Qvale, A., Steier, R., & Sauge, B. (2014, April 2–5). Posing with art: Researching and designing for performative acts of interpretation. In N. Proctor & R. Cherry (Eds.), Paper presented at the *Museums and the web 2014: Proceedings* (pp. 233–248). Baltimore, MD: Museums and the Web, LLC.

Sandoval, W. (2013). Conjecture mapping: An approach to systematic educational design research. *Journal of the Learning Sciences, 23*(1), 18–36.

Yalowitz, S. S., & Bronnenkant, K. (2009). Timing and tracking: Unlocking visitor behavior. *Visitor Studies, 12*(1), 47–64.

10

REFLECTIONS ON DESIGN STORIES

The conclusion to *Design as Scholarship: Case Studies from the Learning Sciences* is told in three parts. First, Janet Kolodner provides a reflection from the learning sciences. Second, Bo Christensen provides a reflection from design studies. Editors Richard Reeve and Vanessa Svihla bring the book to a close with a call for learning scientists to make their design work visible.

Toward Design Practice as a First-Class Research Activity

Janet L. Kolodner

I've been proclaiming for several decades, since I read Ann Brown's design experiment article (1992), that researchers in the learning sciences and their colleagues who are evaluating them for tenure, promotion, and awards need to view design as a first-class research activity. Too many in our field and too many of those evaluating us see design as the work you do to get to the point where you can do "real" research. As editor-in-chief of *The Journal of the Learning Sciences*, I invited articles that would help us learn how to do design, but I found it very hard to get such articles reviewed positively; I often took authors under my wing personally to help them shape their articles so that they would better be appreciated as scholarship, and then I sent them out for review again. Indeed, it was hard for authors to know how to write such articles, as there was not a tradition of doing so. In turn, it was hard for reviewers to know how to review such articles as scholarship. At the National Science Foundation, as lead program officer for the Cyberlearning and Future Learning Technologies program (https://www.nsf.gov/funding/pgm_summ.jsp?pims_id=504984), I had the same experience. The solicitation required investigators to articulate a plan for drawing lessons out of their experiences designing learning technologies, but investigators often had difficulties anticipating the kinds of lessons they might learn and how to recognize the lessons of their designing, and reviewers often had difficulties appreciating and evaluating even well-articulated plans for doing so.

So I am quite pleased that the editors of this book, Vanessa Svihla and Richard Reeve, have pulled together this set of chapters by some of our best designers of learning technologies. These chapters help us understand the kinds of lessons that can be drawn about design as scholarship from those experiences and identify many of the challenges and tensions in taking a scholarly approach to design.

Benefits of Being Scholarly While Engaging in Design

Smith (Chapter 5) points out the affordances of being scholarly about our design work and, hence, the importance of being reflective about design processes as we engage in design work. He refers to Stokes' research quadrants for classifying research goals (Stokes, 1997). Some research, Stokes says, is for purposes of fundamental understanding only, some is purely for purposes of practical or societal use, and some is a combination, focused on fundamental understanding in the context of societal needs, called *Pasteur's Quadrant*. Then there is that fourth quadrant, focused neither on fundamental understanding nor societal need. Stokes did not provide examples of this type of research; he did not imagine scholarship in this quadrant.

For at least the past 2 decades, our field has been claiming that our research, focused on understanding learning in real-world situations and designing for learning and learners, is focused primarily in Pasteur's Quadrant (Barab, 2014). Like Smith, I too have been feeling uncomfortable recently with that classification. It seems like we are often seeking more than simply studying learning and how to affect it in the context of societal need. I think many of our best proposed designs come out of imagining *what is possible* educationally. Smith makes the claim that although we usually begin and end our investigations in Pasteur's Quadrant, our research actually takes us outside that quadrant quite often and into Stokes's fourth quadrant. This scholarship, Smith claims, involves exploring the how-to's and what-if's that eventually allow us to deepen our understanding, broaden our capabilities, and understand better what we actually want or need to achieve.

I don't know whether this is what Stokes intended as the fourth quadrant, but I do agree with Smith that when we learn those things, we should report them so others can benefit from our explorations. Scientists of many types delve into design of new instruments or representations so they can better address issues they've targeted for research. In other fields, those inventions, which often take the form of new instruments and algorithms, are published, are very much appreciated, and allow the field to move forward. For example, advances in the power of microscopes over the years have been essential to the progress of physics, chemistry, and biology. The equivalent for us may be a new way of thinking about a learning environment, an insight into what are the most important constraints or affordances to focus on in design, how a particular kind of interaction with technology might be designed, and I'm sure there are more. Indeed, most of the cases in this book are about such insights.

Affordances of Messiness and Complexity

Ko et al. (Chapter 6) focus on the complexity and messiness of designing for learners when we are aiming to help them master complex skills and practices and when we want learners to understand deeply. Our designs need to anticipate and accommodate the range of starting points of our learners and the different pathways they will take towards capabilities and understanding. They have to anticipate and accommodate, as well, the range of capabilities of teachers and the traditions in different communities and learning environments. And when we approach our designs with an interdisciplinary team, we may find that even agreeing on the learning objectives and on how to interpret observations will necessarily be messy. Ko and colleagues share examples to help us understand that although design discussions will necessarily be messy, they don't have to be unproductive.

Danish and his team (Chapter 3) share how to use activity theory (Engeström, 1987) to help us through such messiness and complexity. The authors tell us such design proceeds best when we think about designing social interactions as a critical and first-class piece of that design. They share two stories about how to use activity theory to do that, showing how the complexities of activity theory that make it seem too difficult to use for design can be used to our advantage. They offer us heuristics about how to cover the space of possibilities while designing learning activities without becoming overwhelmed. A huge methodological insight, indeed!

One of the lessons Teeters, Jurow, and Shea (Chapter 4) teach us in their design story is the value of embedding learning activities into the practices of the users they are designing for. Interestingly, one of the insights Danish's team gleaned from their use of activity theory was the same; finding the activities that are already central to the community and taking advantage of their affordances for designing activity systems that support learning was a very productive tactic for them. My impression is that since this same lesson was extracted from projects with very different foci and very different research approaches, this lesson is particularly powerful.

But Goldman and Jiménez (Chapter 7) teach us just how tricky embedding learning activities into the activities of our users can be. Although they used a rigorous, iterative, and empathy-driven reciprocal research and design process to design socially engaging math games for families, they were not able to dictate the conditions for how, when, and where people would use their apps. They very carefully documented the ways families were interacting (or not) around technology and had family members participate in evaluating and refining the games, but in the end, when left to use the technology themselves, the apps were not adopted. Why not? Possibly because playing math games was not a common way of interacting, or possibly because using technology to interact on road trips was not familiar, use of the technology did not take root as a habit. Perhaps when we want people to take on new habits, we need to take into account as we design how habits are appropriated. That will require collaboration with those who are expert at habit formation and appropriation and will make design considerations even more complex (though hopefully more productive as well).

Pierroux and Steier (Chapter 9) also focus on the affordances of the complexity of designing with interdisciplinary teams. Their group designed a tablet-based tool to help museum staff conduct and analyze observations of visitor behaviors in the museum. As museum staff began to appreciate what was possible, the original design-based research activity was transformed into a research-based design activity, and perspectives on value creation changed considerably. Most interesting, perhaps, is the way institutional practices were transformed through the multiprofessional collaboration.

Making Collaborative Teams Work

Several chapters provide insights about the kinds of collaborators we need on our design teams. How do you decide which ones? How do you find them? How do you keep them? What roles does everyone play? How do you make sure that everyone has a voice? Stieff and Ryan (Chapter 8) discuss how to find the right educators and learners for our design teams. Their chapter teaches us how important it is to recruit broadly for those participants, consider well what each might contribute before inviting them to join the team, compensate them for their time, and break down structural hierarchies so that these participants feel valued.

Teeters, Jurow, and Shea's chapter also discusses this last need. Their chapter contributes a story about what was necessary to integrate community members into their design team and what they had to do to give everyone a voice. Whereas the researchers wanted to learn about the needs and practices of community members, community members thought that they should defer to the researchers. Getting to where everyone understands their role, these researchers tell us, is not always easy but is absolutely necessary. Danish et al.'s chapter also gives insight into the kinds of collaborators we need and the roles they might play. Their team designed the technology in a way that allowed them to easily make changes and then used teachers and students to vet the technology and advise about classroom practices. Goldman and Jiménez also teach about integrating the future users of what we design into our design teams; they used their future users as informants in many of the same ways Teeters et al. and Danish et al. did: to help them understand the conditions under which the technology would be used, understand the social and cultural constraints and affordances of the situations in which their designs would be used, and interpret why designs were not working as well as anticipated and to suggest refinements.

The Challenge of Designing the Future

Others pose challenges or dilemmas. A dilemma that shows itself several times is the issue of how far into the future we are designing. Those designing products for the present day need to involve educators to help them understand classrooms, teachers, and students. But if we want to have an impact in the world, we (learning scientists) need to be reaching beyond designing for the present or even the near future. We need to be leaders helping the public imagine what education could be. How do you design for a future you can't anticipate and when the students and teachers available as collaborators are teachers and students of today? I think the answer is that there are risk-taking educators and institutions today who will work with us. What we imagine as the future of education is pretty closely aligned with what imaginative teachers of today are doing; what we want to do is help them make what they are doing more effective and have them help us design ways of making interesting pedagogical approaches accessible to more educators.

D. Kevin O'Neill (Chapter 2) provides an excellent case of this conundrum in his discussion of the design of the Collaboratory Notebook, an important piece of the larger CoVis project (Edelson, Gordin, & Pea, 1999). The Collaboratory Notebook was an impressive technological achievement for its time (1992). The Internet was not yet in broad use, yet the Collaboratory Notebook allowed teams of students to interact with each other and expert scientists around scientific investigations. The Collaboratory Notebook was not adopted; clearly, a big reason was that the technology was ahead of its time. But that is only part of the story. O'Neill's hindsight tells him that because not enough time was spent on needs assessment, the software was probably too prescriptive in the way it was designed, not giving learners enough freedom in the ways they might contribute to discussions and move forward with their projects. Of course, we didn't know until many years later that we should design for more user freedom. O'Neill's claim is that we may not be able to design for the future. I am more hopeful than he, and my recommendation is to find risk-taking educators to work with.

Taking Advantage of Opportunities

Finally, throughout the chapters, whether made explicit in the writing or not, is an undercurrent of taking advantage of opportunities. My favorite lesson of those Smith teaches us is about why careful observation is so important when we put our work out in the field: such observation affords being pleasantly surprised by what is done with our creations. That practice was critical to his design of

Animal Landlord and to my team's design of Learning by Design (Kolodner et al., 2003). When one takes a designerly approach and is ready to be surprised, opportunities for extending or changing directions arise regularly. But not all opportunities are worth taking on. Each opportunity that arises poses challenges. Some require additional expertise or resources. Some are not practical. Some that are practical may not be worth the time. Pierroux and Steier warn of another trap—transforming a design-based research activity into a research-based design activity. It is not as straightforward as one might think. A team put together for research purposes is not a product development team and vice versa. Pierroux and Steier tell us how they made it work and some of the key differences between design approaches in research and commercial contexts, but they warn that it is not easy work. Their story of how they succeeded in creating a product provides some sobering advice.

My advice: (1) Be aware of when you are thinking about changing course and why. Does the new course of action fit your goals? Are you the right one to do it, or would someone else be the right lead? (2) Think about the team and resources needed to achieve any new goals, as well as the pluses and minuses of following up on opportunities. Make sure you partner correctly to add the right expertise. (3) Think about what it takes for adoption. Is the time right? Is the social situation right? Goldman and Jiménez's team, by all accounts, designed a wonderful family app, but without a community of people ready to buy into it, it could not stand as a product. (4) Finally, be aware of the time, energy, and resources it takes to make a product with any complexity. A researcher might not want to be more than an advisor in making a marketable product. When making learning by design into a product (Project-Based Inquiry Science [PBIS]; http://www.iat.com/courses/middle-school-science/project-based-inquiry-science), I mostly had to divorce myself from research for 2 years to get a product made. If we want to aim toward marketable products, we may very well need to educate our undergraduates, master's students, and some of our PhD students as entrepreneurs, curriculum designers, and technology integrators.

Closing Thoughts

Designing effective curriculum and learning technologies is difficult and complex; we need to design not just for the average learner, but rather in ways that address all learners. We need to address "worldly needs," as Svihla and Reeve tell us in their introduction, as well as conceptual needs. We cannot do that without learning each other's design lessons, becoming intimate with the "design patterns" that others have used, and becoming aware of each other's failures. If we can collect enough information about the success and failure of different design patterns and approaches, we will eventually be able to explain why each works (or doesn't) and know how and when to use them. If we are to become better designers of learning activities and technologies, and indeed, if we want our designs to have an impact, we will need to treat design as a first-class research activity, report our design insights and failures for others to learn from, and make it a habit to be "designerly" as we work. Essentially, we must make building on the design insights and design patterns of others standard habits of our field. I hope the insights reported in the chapters of this book will help us move in those directions.

Iterations on a Designerly Science

Bo T. Christensen

This set of chapters is written by courageous scholars willing to admit they are both designers and learning scientists at the same time. Through the challenge set by editors Svihla and Reeve, we have been invited (in the words of some of the authors) "under the hood" of the learning sciences. Here we witness second-hand that the process of generating and testing learning science theory is much more "designerly" than is readily reported in the final published scientific papers. The invitation seems to suggest that the machinery of design is somehow incompatible with—or at least somewhat controversial in relation to—the machinery of science. This reflection aims to explore how the book chapters contribute to the science/design "controversy," as seen through the lens of the design studies literature. The paradox is that science generates knowledge using means that are not designerly in nature, but to design viable tools and interventions, learning scientists must engage in designing as it is practiced in the design disciplines.

The obvious choice of a starting point is the design studies recent classic "Designerly ways of knowing" (2006) by Nigel Cross, where the historical controversies between design and science are unfolded. Cross argues that the science of design is the study of design, which leaves open the interpretation of the nature of design, and concludes that

> the science of design refers to that body of work which attempts to improve our understanding of design through "scientific" (i.e., systematic, reliable) methods of investigation. And let us be clear that a "science of design" is not the same as a "design science," which is "an explicitly organized, rational and wholly systematic approach to design."
>
> (p. 123)

Cross argues that the science of design is the study of "designerly ways of knowing." He moves on to point out that there is some confusion or controversy over the nature of design research, but argues through the works of Bruce Archer (1981) that good research (and thus also good design research) is purposive, inquisitive, informed, methodological, and communicable, and that these characteristics are normal features of good research in any discipline.

Because we may readily study designerly processes through scientific methods, one could be led to believe that the controversy between design and science is now resolved. So then where does this design/science apprehension come from—what's the fuss? Believing that the establishment of a design research discipline proper resolves the issue, however, would be missing the key point of this book: a practiced designerly *process* may sometimes seem incompatible with a scientific investigation. Although designers and scientists both create knowledge, there may well be devils in the details of how they do so, hence the controversy. Designerly processes are characterized, for example, by iterations, collaborative participation, and the "wickedness" of the problems approached. A prime example of a still controversial aspect of a designerly scientific method is exactly this iterative nature of the design process, addressed in every chapter of this book.

To illustrate why an iterative process might be conceived of as controversial from a scientific methods standpoint, try for a second to foreground your knowledge of statistics. How does "iterative statistical testing" of some hypothesis sound? On the one hand, it could mean rigorous testing as in attempts at replication, which would be all fine and good. But on the other hand, it could also mean repeating tests again and again with slight variations in order to get the result you want. The latter would, of course, not be the best of scientific practices (see Simmons, Nelson & Simonsohn, 2011), in that repeated procedures are likely to bring about significant differences at some point—not because there is actually a difference to be found, but simply due to statistical conventions of a 5% significance level whereby 1 in 20 tests—by chance—will get you a significant difference where there actually is no difference. Reporting only on the final iteration ("final form") may thus not always seem like the best of scientific practices if the purpose is to test a theory. Or try instead to view the concept of iteration from the perspective of the philosophy of science scholar Karl Popper (1963); in the hypothetico-deductive method, one should make bold conjectures, deduce hypotheses, and then rigorously attempt to refute or falsify them. An iterative process may immunize the theory from refutation by embedding the falsifying observation into the theory. Such iterative (learning) processes are seen as problematic, in that they circumvent falsification in order to save the hypothesis and thereby potentially limit scientific progress. Similar concerns are sometimes raised against artificial intelligence (AI) models whereby a large number of iterative learning cycles on some dataset may tweak the model to mirror the dataset, but may not prove to be a valid model beyond this. From such scientific perspectives, designerly iterations may give cause for concern!

One of the most defining characteristics of a designerly approach is that in creative design, the design problem and potential solutions "co-evolve" through a series of iterations (Dorst & Cross, 2001; Kolodner & Willis, 1996; Maher, 1994). Through iterative co-evolution, not only do potential design solutions receive consideration in the context of the requirements that define the problem, but such requirements can also themselves be adapted in the light of novel solution attempts. Design problems (including the design of learning interventions and research designs) are not fixed problems to be solved along the lines of traditional problem-solving models (e.g., Newell & Simon, 1972). Rather, through iterative processes, problem–solution pairings (or bridges) may be formed as a result of exploring and changing the nature of the problem and the solution. In real-world empirical investigations, co-evolution has been linked to creative activities such as analogizing and mental simulation in collaborative design teams (Wiltschnig, Christensen, & Ball, 2013). Interestingly, scientific discovery has also been proposed as taking place through a dual search in two problem spaces: a hypothesis space and an experiment space that interact with each other (Klahr & Dunbar, 1988). The similarity of the scientific discovery as dual search model and the theory of co-evolution in design is striking, suggesting that the iterative co-evolution of problem and solution may not be specific to design.

The making of interventions and research designs is, however, a creative endeavor or wicked problem in its own right, and needs to be designed. As argued by Glynn (1985), "[I]t is the epistemology of design that has inherited the task of developing the logic of creativity, hypothesis innovation or invention that has proved so elusive to the philosophers of science" (pp. 125–126). Although it may be possible to argue in general terms from theory how a learning intervention or a research design should look in a particular research project, many of the devilish details cannot be deduced directly and are only discovered through iterative trial and error, as empirically oriented scientists will be aware. Still (as put by one of the most creative and prolific professors in the learning sciences I know) given the format of scientific journals, we get to pretend that we deduced everything and knew all along when we write up the study.

The development of the projects reported in this volume may be viewed as creative attempts at reaching a problem–solution pairing through co-evolution iterations. For example, in the chapter by Smith, the original concept in BGuILE changed radically through the iterative development of software for high school biology classrooms. Through a series of iterations, user input and serendipitous remarks by colleagues fundamentally changed a piece of software entitled Animal Landlord from an initial lion hunting simulation utilizing an aerial view of the Serengeti, through combining the watching of an actual video clip with a later simulated model, to finally abandoning the original simulation to instead rely on multiple case videos.

Several of the chapters tackle head on how their initial abstract and research-based design principles evolved over time through iterations with attempted solutions (e.g., Stieff & Ryan; O'Neill; Goldman & Jiménez).

Between the lines, one may detect in some of the chapters a certain longing for the sufficiency of analysis: if only analyzing and deducing from theory in itself would bring about a design, that would make the designerly research efforts seem much more like how you write up "proper" research and less like creative design. As the concept of the co-evolution of problem space and solution space informs us, there *is* a certain gap to be creatively filled: all the analysis in the world of the research problem space will not be deducible to a mere singular designed solution—the researchers need to take a designerly leap of faith in bridging the two. The vocabulary on that leap differs between chapters, but the creative nondeductive leap of faith seems clear: opportunism, educated guesses or design serendipity (Smith), trial and error (Stieff & Ryan), brainstorming (Goldman & Jiménez; Danish, Enyedy, Saleh, & Lee), and tweaking (Pierroux & Steier) are some of the terms used. In the words of Goldman and Jiménez, we need to somehow *translate* the research findings or design principles into design solutions through a series of steps. In that translation process, it may be worth considering whether the design principles can serve as what Darke (1979) dubbed "primary generators" where an understanding of the problem is gained by testing conjectured solutions. "Principles" should thus not be mistaken for immutable problem boundaries as in the "classic" problem-solving sense, but rather seen as generative for solution conjectures in an iterative process.

The need for problem framing is discussed in some of the chapters with a theoretical orientation towards cultural historical activity theory (CHAT). If theories could be placed on a continuum of how many variables they attempt to incorporate, CHAT would probably be placed at the more "complex" end. The chapter by Teeters, Jurow, and Shea, for example, approached a particular high-level design challenge of developing methods for doing equity-oriented research (i.e., research and design efforts that facilitate members of marginalized communities in gaining greater access to and control over resources to shape their own lives). A certain amount of theoretical reconceptualization, or self-imposed theoretical simplification, may help avoid getting lost in the quagmire of possibilities set by such problems, as when Danish et al. report how an ever-expanding sequence of CHAT triangles were reconceptualized more simply into how the activity of play transformed into the activity of scientific modeling. In other chapters, we also find direct examples of how solution conjectures lead to reformulation of the problem space. O'Neill describes the development of the Collaborative Notebook, highlighting how certain key assumptions and central design decisions led to the implementation of a user interface that disallowed normal user behavior and alienated their original target audience. The design failure is mainly attributed to the lack of a proper needs assessment of the target audience. Nonetheless, although not useful for their original target audience (K–12 teachers), the novel design did manage to find other more suitable audiences in other contexts (problem-based learning at medical schools, and literary support among African-American students). O'Neill describes these later attempts at finding new audiences for their software as a trap of "desperation for success" that should instead have been met with the acceptance of failure, and attempts to report this design failure. However, when seen from the perspective of co-evolution of problem and solution, the teams' actions to recontextualize the software appear to be perfectly valid attempts at finding a learning problem fitting their novel solution. Indeed, the software did appear to match other contexts much better than the original target audience, and it is only by maintaining that the software was designed to solve a single fixed problem that it could be seen as a failure. This is not to say that scholars should not *also* report design failures as encouraged by O'Neill (after all, the *desk-drawer problem* of never-reported null results needs to be taken seriously in science), but rather to say that there may be a multitude of creativity in opening up the *problem* space and rethinking what exactly the software may have to offer in other problem contexts. That path should not be seen as a guilt-ridden path of desperation! The creative potential in finding new functions to preexisting forms (aka the form-before-function approach to design) is well documented in both laboratory studies (Finke, Ward, & Smith, 1992) and in real-world design situations (Ball & Christensen, 2009). My most frequently used warm-up exercise for brainstorming sessions illustrates the potential: "The manager of a Ping-Pong ball factory has accidentally overinflated his latest shipment, rendering the balls unusable for regular table tennis. What might be all the ways you can use 10,000 overinflated Ping-Pong balls?" Most groups will have no problem producing 15 novel ideas in a mere 3-minute session. What creative waste if we were to only think of the overinflation as a manufacturing failure. Fortunately, creative desperation proved the mother of invention also for O'Neill, as the design found new audiences. Similar stories can be found throughout this volume: Pierroux and Steier report on the development of VisiTracker—a tablet-based research tool and online portal for museum curators that proved highly useful in a multitude of other contexts as well, which challenged the research team in the borderlands between research and entrepreneurship. Further, problem redefinition is not limited to contextual shifting, as evidenced in Ko et al. The development of READI proved to be a process where a key artifact—evidence and interpretation charts—co-evolved with the team's conceptual understanding, diverging from an initial universal model through numerous iterations to a domain-specific one, where the literature team, the history team, and the science team utilized the charts in different ways.

Hopefully, these case stories will help the rest of us realize that when doing designerly research, creative leaps and co-evolutionary iterations are necessary, both on the path from theory to design and as crucial parts of the learning sciences.

Designing: The Unseen Dimension of Our Scholarship

Richard Reeve and Vanessa Svihla

In the preface, Tim Koschmann encouraged us to attend to the "Shop Floor Problem" in order to better understand the place of design in our work. On the most basic level, our goal in making the call for chapters for this book was to reassure ourselves that, indeed, design *is* part of our scholarship. We were rewarded with an impressive array of chapter proposals that spoke strongly to the wide range of approaches to designing that are being used in our field. We believe Koschmann also rightly proposed the key issue in beginning to examine design in our work is that of *documentation*. The authors of the selected chapters have taken up this call by documenting, in significant and sometimes painful detail, the design processes they engaged in as they developed a range of learning technologies and innovative approaches for learning.

Several other insights arose from the design stories. Janet Kolodner noted that the current publication environment may have had the effect of limiting our reporting about our designing, especially where projects have failed, at least initially, to meet proposed expectations. Bo Christensen, speaking from the design studies field, raised the concern that design may be not be as prevalent or at least as visible in the work of learning scientists due to a perceived conflict between the epistemologies of science and design.

Here, we take up what we view as potentially intractable dualisms that have been put forward in the book: documentation and publication, design processes and frameworks, failure and the future, and scholarship and design. In each case, we review the situation and present a potential path for moving forward so designing can indeed be an overt part of our scholarship as learning scientists, or as D. Kevin O'Neill positioned it, as "scholar-designers."

Documentation and Publication

A basic premise of this book was that, based on depictions from our final-form publications, *design* in the learning sciences appeared to be quite different from how it is generally practiced in the allied design fields (e.g., architecture, engineering, fashion design). Further, it seemed our design practices had not come from these fields but instead emerged from scientific ways of working; thus, in reporting our results, the processes of science have taken priority over the processes of design. We found that these stories of designing, finally considered in earnest by the researchers, rendered a process that was much more emergent, contextual, and iterative than had been shared in their previously published work. We see this as a *blind spot* in our work that will be fruitful to address, as it hides important possibilities and insights in the work of our community. Moreover, we view improved documentation, and thereby better attention to the mundane details of our work, as essential to engaging in more designerly activity and for improving communication about the nature of design in our work.

The chapter authors reported how difficult, yet rewarding, it was to write their design stories. For authors who had originally carefully set out to document their design process, this was easier to accomplish. Good documentation was a source of essential information that supported their (re)viewing of the events (e.g., O'Neill). Goldman and Ko reported going back to the teachers to ask if their software had worked for the users. Good documentation helped them go back to those decisions and reflect on the question of usefulness. However, there are few obvious incentives to careful documentation of our design work, as we seldom have the opportunity to share it as scholarship. Thus, others pieced their design stories together from memory, backed by limited original sources, such as notes, manuscript drafts, and e-mails.

Authors noted they viewed this as a valuable undertaking, but that it was not something they were accustomed to doing in their typical reporting practices. We hope telling these stories can help the field recognize traditional final-form publication as incomplete and as unsatisfying; when research involving the design of new learning tools and processes is presented as a linear process, we hope readers remain hungry for the design story, for the details of iteration and contingency, that readers become adept at exercising a healthy dose of skepticism about processes reported as linear, if not the results themselves. By telling these stories, which detail previously *unseen* insights into the processes in which authors engaged, some authors found possibilities for future work they themselves had not previously seen. This was the case for O'Neill over 20 years after the project had finished. This speaks to the value of formally yet honestly sharing our design stories.

The design stories also provide a reality check that makes designing more accessible; they depict the design process as iterative and emergent, as noted by Christensen in his commentary. For less experienced scholar-designers, this may well be a revelation and one that is needed to ensure they persevere in the face of failures and nonlinear challenges of designing. Too often, our work is depicted as proceeding in a rational, linear fashion. In the absence of an awareness of the nonlinear reality of designing, they may have thought themselves imposters or incapable of doing design because they couldn't seem to attain the linear perfection so often reported in publications.

As Janet Kolodner points out, grant proposals require us to present our planned design work in a rational, logical form; yet the design stories in this book suggest that our actual work is in fact iterative and emergent. In essence, our funding and publication mechanisms guide us to say one thing—in the service of giving life to our projects from a funding and promotion point of view—but then do something else to actually accomplish our projects. Kolodner implores us to begin to view design "as a first-class research activity," yet it continues to be unseen in our publications. We hope that this volume will help encourage this perception of detailed documentation as design scholarship.

Design Processes and Frameworks

Across the set of stories, we see productive tensions between engaging in design processes and reliance on frameworks, whether these are scholarly (e.g., conceptual frameworks, methodological lenses, principles) or agenda driven (e.g., following the *Common Guidelines for Education Research and Development* [Institute of Education Sciences, U.S. Department of Education, & National Science Foundation, 2013], driving an innovation to scale).

Several of the design stories recount issues with the viability of designs when the authors didn't take sufficient time to understand the needs, concerns, and desires of their "clients" or contexts. Balancing these needs with the goal of "inventing the future," as O'Neill positioned it, seems to be the sticking point for our work. We don't suggest that design offers us an easy solution to this problem; it is in many ways the "wicked problem" (Rittel & Webber, 1973) of our field. It suggests a need for taking a problematizing stance on both the solution *and* the problem. It requires a willingness to live with what can be an extended period of ambiguity during the design phases of the work. Certainly, at some point, there needs to be a move to *fix* or *firm up* the problem and solution for presentation and reporting purposes, but we argue that often this happens too early in our work.

In recounting their design efforts, some authors have found it important to use some form of external academic framework to assist in explaining their design decisions (e.g., Danish et al.; Ko et al., Goldman & Jiménez). We suspect this desire comes from our common concern that designing isn't well understood and therefore needs to be explained in connection to other academic literature. But we also wonder if it stems from a collective preference to avoid ambiguity. We certainly understand the desire for certainty, but it is instructive that the significant forward movements in the projects reported in this book occurred when the design process was marked by a tangible openness to the problem–solution space. For instance, some authors began with one problem, but ended with another (e.g., Smith; Pierroux & Steier). Ko and colleagues reported the problem of students seeing claims and evidence as the same thing. In iteratively seeking to address this, they remarked "We know we aren't going to get it right the first time." This recognition of the necessity of prototyping in context acknowledges the malleability of the process and the outcome. This suggests that where develop principles too early in the process, we may end up precluding possible avenues for both solution and problem advancement. Design principles, at least those generated early in the process, may be more appropriately conceived as design features or conjectures to be worked with as prop... ... for action, bearing in mind that these belong to one *possible and tentat...* lution, not the (final) solution. More to the point, any prototype, in adva... the one that we settle on, should be regarded more for its ability to gen... sight into the problem itself. This problem-first stance may help guard... what, in the design literature, is regarded as a novice move to fixate... single solution too early in the process (Jansson & Smith, 1991). But it... way to help us understand our design work as scholarly.

We hope that by recognizing our design... ...s scholarly, we can rely less upon frameworks and experiment more... ...ner, more agile approach to designing. Here we propose that the k... ...king a designerly stance; this would entail acknowledging problems... ...ckedly embedded in the world (e.g., Goldman & Jiménez; Smith; Teeters, Jurow, & Shea) such that contextual constraints and client needs must be attended to *directly*, not solely via scholarly means. This would also mean taking comfort, wallowing even, in the ambiguity of problem framing/solution refining, thus allowing the problem and solution to oscillate, even to the point of treating the most promising problem–solution pairing as problematic. It would mean acknowledging that collaboration is vital but problematic in and of itself, and can pull our designing into unfamiliar realms (Pierroux & Steier); it can reveal challenging power dynamics (Teeters, Jurow, & Shea; Stieff & Ryan) or show us how challenging it can be to find a problem we can agree on (Ko et al.). Taking a designerly stance means treating prototyping as a way to gain insights into the problem (e.g., Smith) by testing them in contextualized ways (Stieff & Ryan; O'Neill). Ultimately, it's not about "the" design process—it's about taking a designerly stance.

Such designerly approaches, based on the chapters in this book, are clearly part of our work; thus, we challenge learning scientists to honor this designerly stance by more fully conveying the nuances of what led to their solutions and how their problems may have changed over time. We anticipate that taking this approach will lead to a future that isn't, as O'Neill suggested "built the night before it is due," but one that emerges out of a concerted effort to engage in iterative problem framing and solution refining over an extended period.

Failure and the Future

O'Neill suggests we need new scholarly norms for reporting "failures" like those he contends were part of the work he reports on in his chapter. In her commentary, Kolodner suggests that this work should be seen from the perspective of helping to move forward the entire project of which O'Neill's work was a part, as well as offering insight for future projects. We support this view, but further suggest that we would do well to view *all* learning sciences projects, and perhaps especially those that ostensibly report failures, as contributing to our collective advancement. Poski (1992) notes that "failures always teach us more than successes about the design of things. And thus the failures often lead to redesigns—to new, improved things" (Petroski, 1992, p. 49). In contrast, when we focus only on our successes we mask weaknesses in our designs that can ultimately lead to catastrophic failures (Petroski, 1992).

In the conclusion chapter, O'Neill cites the example of the *Issy les Moulineaux* public parade in Paris where early aeronautical designers went to test their aircrafts for all. As he put it, "failures informed everyone." Kolodner takes up this point in her commentary, suggesting we need to find those "risk-taking educators and learners" that are imaginative and interested in helping to invent the futures. We applaud this directive but wonder where we should go to find these risk-takers. A tension that comes through in the chapters is the difficulty authors had in recruiting and working with their collaborative design teams in order to begin and sustain the invention process (e.g., Teeters, Jurow, & Shea; Stieff & Ryan; Pierroux & Steier).

We suggest there may be qualities of spaces that make them particularly good spaces in which to test our prototypes of the future, gathering insights about our problems in the same way the French aeronautical designers did on the parade field. To consider what such spaces might need to look like to serve this function, we consider an example: the space just beside the workshop at the Exploratorium, a world-renowned science and technology museum in San Francisco. The Exploratorium positioned the workshop—the place where exhibits are built—right beside the entrance and in full view of the public. This placement was no accident. When the Exploratorium moved in 2013 from its original location at the Palace of Fine Arts to its current location on Pier 15, the workshop was placed in exactly the same location. This placement is important to their work, as they often set prototypes out so the flow of guests can interact with them and provide feedback about the design. Then they take the exhibit back to continue with their design work. The technicians view iteration and feedback as central to their work (Socolofsky, 2012). In this example, we see the opportunity for lean design, making many iterative cycles feasible to accomplish. We wonder if maker spaces could similarly serve as a setting to test new innovations, if learning scientists, embedded in such spaces, might not be able to similarly bring prototype designs to participants for feedback.

Often, our designs for learning require extended periods of engagement, and testing a component of a longer design might not provide information about how it will function in situ. Finding test beds for the future was a concern for John Dewey more than a century ago, when in 1896 he proposed the creation of a school as part of the newly formed Department of Pedagogy at the University of Chicago. For Dewey, the key was that the school would be a place where what was *possible* in education would be explored. He wrote to the president of the university:

> The conduct of a school of demonstration, observation and experiment in connection with the theoretical instruction is the nerve of the whole scheme. Without this no pedagogical department can command the confidence of the educational public it is seeking to lay hold of and direct; the mere profession of principles without their practical exhibition and testing will not engage the respect of the educational profession. Without it, the theoretical work partakes of the nature of a farce and imposture—it is like neglecting to provide a laboratory for faculty and students to work in.
>
> *(Dewey, 1896a, p. 434)*

Separately, he stated: "[I]t is the function of some schools to provide better teachers according to present standards; it is the function of others to create new standards and ideals and thus to lead to a gradual change in conditions"

(Dewey, 1896b, p. 437). Laboratory schools have the *potential* to provide the kind of institutional setting Kolodner is requesting, though many such schools have instead become focused on the preparation of the teachers of today (National Association of laboratory Schools, 1991; Tanner, 1997). In some places, charter schools may provide forward-thinking test fields. However, many schools, in the face of teacher de-professionalization, high-stakes assessment, and teacher evaluation become risk averse. This risk aversion is decidedly not a characteristic of a promising test bed for the future, yet it is an all-too-common characteristic of the present, and we are reminded of Ann Brown's concern that our designs should endure the stress test of the "blooming, buzzing confusion" of the classroom (1992, p. 2). An approach used in adjacent fields is to cultivate a group of empathic users (Lin & Seepersad, 2007) or bring users into the design process through participatory design (Yip et al., 2013). This aligns with the approaches taken by Stieff and Ryan and by Teeters, Jurow, and Shea, who show how central building trust and overcoming power imbalances are to having access to iterative feedback in our work.

Scholarship and Design

Koschmann suggested in the preface that our goal as learning scientists isn't just to design products for instruction, but to inquire into the value of these goals themselves. Smith and Kolodner both referenced Stokes's "Quadrant Model of Scientific Research" (1997), noting that there is designerly work that isn't necessarily use-inspired nor immediately pursuing new knowledge, and therefore that doesn't fit into the three named quadrants (Bohr's pure basic research, Edison's pure applied research, and Pasteur's use-inspired basic research). Smith positioned this in what he terms the fourth quadrant, which in Stokes's model is unnamed. Stokes referenced research by Comroe and Dripps (1978) who found that 17% of the medical technology research studies they reviewed didn't fall into the three main categories of the model; they were classified as "development" studies, which could be deemed low on both knowledge and use, and oriented toward *what is possible*. Stokes described the fourth quadrant as including "research that systematically explores *particular* phenomena without having in view either general explanatory objectives or any applied use to which the results will be put" (Stokes, 1997, p. 74, emphasis in original). We would add "right away" to the end of this statement, as we think this fits with the way Smith and Kolodner are representing the moves designers sometimes make when they explore the potential of certain tools, without, at that moment, a particular use in mind. This seems to be what Danish and colleagues were doing when they began to work with motion-tracking technology and described it as "technology in search of a use."

We also think that our work as scholar-designers extends well past this fourth quadrant, and could result in three related publications. First, we would suggest the kind of careful, ethnographic work undertaken to understand the context could result in a publication that would sit within Bohr's pure basic research quadrant. In fact, Goldman and Jiménez refer to this part of their design story as "basic research." Second, we would argue the findings from testing a design in a study (or sequence of studies) would fit within Pasteur's use-inspired basic research quadrant. Finally, a design story, such as told in this volume, would fit within Edison's pure applied research quadrant.

Closing Thoughts

The chapters in this book attest to the difficulty, value, and potential of attending to the details of our designing. When designing had not been well documented, telling the design story became harder. The authors commented on the value they saw in working through the retelling of the design work as it related to the intervention and tools they had developed. Several also commented on the importance of attending to the details of the design work as it was a more honest rendering of the process they had engaged in. We view this as a key contribution to the field. Especially for those new to the learning sciences, these stories provide a more honest depiction of our work, which is more commonly shown as a rational, linear process. Instead, these forthright reflections signal the importance of emergence, contingency, and a willingness to be comfortable with ambiguity for our work.

Stenhouse has said that research is "systematic inquiry made public" (1983, p. 185). If design is part of our scholarship, then it must be made visible. We believe a volume such as this, where the nature of design in our work is revealed and examined, is an excellent starting point.

References

Archer, B. (1981). A view of the nature of design research. In R. Jacques & J. Powell, (Eds.), *Design: Science: Method*. Guildford, UK: Westbury House.

Ball, L.J., & Christensen, B.T. (2009). Analogical reasoning and mental simulation in design: Two strategies linked to uncertainty resolution. *Design Studies, 30*(2), 169–186.

Barab, S. (2014). Design-based research. In R. Keith Sawyer (Ed.), *The Cambridge handbook of the learning sciences: A methodological toolkit for the learning scientist* (2nd ed., pp. 153–170). New York, NY: Cambridge University Press.

Brown, A.L. (1992). Design experiments: Theoretical and methodological challenges in creating complex interventions in classroom settings. *The Journal of the Learning Sciences, 2*(2), 141–178. doi:10.1207/s15327809jls0202_2.

Comroe, J.H., Jr. & Dripps, R.D. (1978). Scientific basis for the support of biomedical science. In H.H. Fudenberg & V.L. Melnick (Eds.), *Biomedical scientists and public policy* (pp. 15–33). New York, NY: Springer.

Cross, N. (2006). *Designerly ways of knowing*. London: Springer.

Darke, J. (1979). The primary generator and the design process. *Design Studies, 1*(1), 36–44.

Dewey, J. (1896a). The need for a laboratory school. In J.A. Boyston (Ed.), *John Dewey: The early works (1882–1898) Vol. 5* (pp. 433–435) Carbondale, IL: The Southern Illinois University Press.

Dewey, J. (1896b). The university school. *University Record (University of Chicago), 1*, 417–419.

Dorst, K., & Cross, N. (2001). Creativity in the design process: Co-evolution of problem-solution. *Design Studies, 22*(5), 425–437.

Edelson, D., Gordin, D., & Pea, R.D. (1999). Addressing the challenges of inquiry-based learning through technology and curriculum design. *Journal of the Learning Sciences, 8*(3), 391–450.

Engeström, Y. (1987). *Learning by expanding: An activity-theoretical approach to developmental research.* Helsinki: Orienta-Konsultit Oy.

Finke, R.A., Ward, T.B., & Smith, S.M. (1992). *Creative cognition: Theory, research, and applications.* Cambridge, MA: MIT Press.

Glynn, S. (1985). Science and perception as design. *Design Studies, 6*(3), 122–126.

Institute of Education Sciences, U.S. Department of Education, & National Science Foundation. (2013). *Common guidelines for education research and development.* Retrieved from http://www.nsf.gov/pubs/2013/nsf13126/nsf13126.pdf

Jansson, D.G., & Smith, S.M. (1991). Design fixation. *Design Studies, 12*(1), 3–11.

Klahr, D., & Dunbar, K. (1988). Dual space search during scientific reasoning. *Cognitive Science, 12*(1), 1–48.

Kolodner, J.L., Camp, P.J., Crismond, D., Fasse, B.B., Gray, J., Holbrook, J.K., . . . Ryan, M. (2003). Problem-based learning meets case-based reasoning in the middle-school science classroom: Putting learning-by-design into practice. *Journal of the Learning Sciences, 12*(4), 495–547.

Kolodner, J.L., & Willis, L.M. (1996). Powers of observation in creative design. *Design Studies, 17*(4), 385–416.

Lin, J., & Seepersad, C.C. (2007). Empathic lead users: The effects of extraordinary user experiences on customer needs analysis and product redesign. In proceedings of *ASME 2007 international design engineering technical conferences and computers and information in engineering conference Volume 3: 19th International Conference on Design Theory and Methodology.* Las Vegas, NV: ASME.

Maher, M.L. (1994). Creative design using a genetic algorithm. *Proceedings of computing in civil engineering,* pp. 2014–2021. New York, NY: American Society of Civil Engineers.

National Association of laboratory Schools. (1991). *Laboratory schools: An educational resource.* Manoa, HI: University of Hawaii, Curriculum Research & Development Group.

Newell, A., & Simon, H.A. (1972). *Human problem solving.* Englewood Cliffs, NJ: Prentice-Hall.

Petroski, H. (1992). *To engineer is human: The role of failure in successful design.* New York, NY: Vintage books.

Popper, K. (1963). *Conjectures and refutations: The growth of scientific knowledge.* London: Routledge.

Rittel, H.W.J., & Webber, M.M. (1973). Dilemmas in a general theory of planning. *Policy Sciences, 4*(2), 155–169.

Simmons, J.P., Nelson, L.D., & Simonsohn, U. (2011). False-positive psychology: Undisclosed flexibility in data collection and analysis allows presenting anything as significant. *Psychological Science, 22*(11), 1359–1366.

Socolofsky, E. (2012). Iterating for visitors at the Exploratorium. *UX Magazine*. Retrieved from https://uxmag.com/articles/iterating-for-visitors-at-the-exploratorium

Stenhouse, L. (1983). *Authority, emancipation and education*. London: Heinemann.

Stokes, D.E. (1997). *Pasteur's quadrant: Basic science and technological innovation*. Washington, DC: Brookings Institution Press.

Tanner, L.N. (1997). *Dewey's laboratory school: Lessons for today*. New York: Teachers College Press.

Wiltschnig, S., Christensen, B. T., & Ball, L. (2013). Collaborative problem-solution co-evolution in creative design. *Design Studies, 34*(5), 515–542.

Yip, J., Clegg, T., Bonsignore, E., Gelderblom, H., Rhodes, E., & Druin, A. (2013). Brownies or bags-of-stuff?: Domain expertise in cooperative inquiry with children. Paper presented at the *Proceedings of the 12th international conference on interaction design and children*, New York, NY: ACM.

LIST OF CONTRIBUTORS' NAMES AND AFFILIATIONS

Michael Bolz, University of Illinois at Chicago
Bo T. Christensen, Copenhagen Business School
Joshua Danish, Indiana University
Noel Enyedy, University of California, Los Angeles
MariAnne George, University of Illinois at Chicago
Shelley Goldman, Stanford University
Susan R. Goldman, University of Illinois at Chicago
Allison Hall, University of Illinois at Chicago
Katherine James, University of Illinois at Chicago
Osvaldo Jiménez, University of the Pacific
A. Susan Jurow, University of Colorado Boulder
Mon-Lin Ko, University of Illinois at Chicago
Janet L. Kolodner, Concord Consortium
Timothy Koschmann, Southern Illinois University
Christine Lee, University of California, Los Angeles
D. Kevin O'Neill, Simon Fraser University
Palmyre Pierroux, University of Oslo
Jacquelynn Popp, University of Illinois at Chicago
Joshua Radinsky, University of Illinois at Chicago
Richard Reeve, Queen's University
Stephanie Ryan, American Institutes for Research
Asmalina Saleh, Indiana University
Molly Shea, Exploratorium
Brian K. Smith, Drexel University
Rolf Steier, University of Oslo
Mike Stieff, University of Illinois at Chicago
Vanessa Svihla, University of New Mexico
Leah Teeters, University of Colorado Boulder

INDEX